ONE SHINING SEASON

The amazing story of Michigan State University's 1998-99 men's basketball team

Lansing State Journal

News You Can Use
www.greenandwhite.com

SPORTS PUBLISHING INC.
www.SportsPublishingInc.com

ACKNOWLEDGMENTS

The 1998-99 Michigan State Spartans won more games (33) than any other Big Ten team in history, including an incredible 22 straight victories in their run to the NCAA Final Four.

During this record-setting season, the *Lansing State Journal* gave its readers a front-row seat for every game. Bringing these events to the pages of the *State Journal* required hard work and dedication on the part of many reporters, columnists, editors, executives, and photographers at the newspaper. Among those who were instrumental in assisting us in this project were Steve Crosby, Byron Roberts, Rich Adams and Shawn Joslyn. From the *State Journal* sports pages, we specifically want to acknowledge the contributions of Gerry Ahern, Jack Ebling, Larry Lage, Tom Gantert, Todd Schulz, Rod Sanford, Greg DeRuiter, Robert Killips, Kathy Kieliszewski, David Olds, and Chris Holmes.

Sports Publishing Inc.

©1999 *The Lansing State Journal*
All rights reserved. The reprinted articles and photographs were originally published in *The Lansing State Journal.* In some instances, articles appearing in this book have been edited to accommodate certain space limitations. However, wherever possible, we have included the articles in their entirety. All photographs are provided by *Lansing State Journal* photographers Rod Sandford, Greg DeRuiter, Robert Killips, Kathy Kieliszewski, David Olds, and Chris Holmes except for the photographs on pages 10, 13, and 29, which were provided by AP/Wide World Photos.

Sports Publishing Inc. staff: Joseph J. Bannon, Jr.,
  Michael G. Pearson, Joanna L. Wright,
  Terrence C. Miltner, and Claudia Mitroi
Editor: Susan M. McKinney
Interior design: Terry N. Hayden
Book Layout: Terry N. Hayden, Susan M. McKinney,
  Jennifer L. Polson and Erin J. Prescher
Cover Design: Terry N. Hayden

ISBN: 1-58261-131-9
Library of Congress Number: 99-62297

Printed in the United States.

SPORTS PUBLISHING INC.
www.SportsPublishingInc.com

TABLE OF CONTENTS

ACKNOWLEDGMENTS............ ii

INTRODUCTION iv

NON-CONFERENCE GAMES.. 2

BIG TEN SEASON 20

BIG TEN TOURNAMENT 56

NCAA ROUND 1 64

NCAA ROUND 2 66

NCAA ROUND 3 70

NCAA ROUND 4 76

FINAL FOUR 84

Introduction

'98 Was Good to Spartans, '99 Even Better?

• • • • • • • • • • • • • •

EAST LANSING—So long, 1998.

It wasn't the year Tom Izzo wanted.

Nothing less than perfection could be.

But 24 wins and eight losses should send an unmistakable message.

Overall, it was a very good 12 months for the Michigan State men's basketball program.

And with continued recruiting success, there is more good news.

It might be just the beginning of sweet memories to come.

Last December 31, the Spartans were 8-3 after an upset at Purdue but less than three weeks removed from "Izzo must go!" conversation.

After losses to Illinois-Chicago, Temple and Detroit, a lot of fans were beginning to wonder.

Today, with a 10-3 mark after a trouncing of UNC-Asheville Wednesday night, that same MSU program is considered one of the nation's best.

Even if this team is an extra ballhandler or another big man away from national title contention, it's a group no coach will want to face in March.

And it could signal the start of something bigger.

Something to talk about 20 years from now.

Hello, 1999.

–Jack Ebling
December 31, 1998

• • • • • • • • • • • • • •

Road to the Final Four
Non-Conference Games

PRESSING THE ISSUE

NOVEMBER 11, 1998
LARRY LAGE

EAST LANSING—The Michigan State basketball team has received plenty of preseason press.

The Spartans are heralded as the nation's second-best team by Basketball Times, No. 4 by USA TODAY/ESPN and fifth by The Associated Press.

Now, it's time they pressed. Plenty.

We're talking full-court, man-to-man defensive pressure.

Why?

The Spartans are at their best when they're running, and full-court pressure would ensure that happens more often.

That fact was evident in MSU's 101-79 exhibition win over Athletes in Action on Tuesday night at the Breslin Center.

> "We could really wear down teams if we pressed, and I know point guards would hate to have a guy in their face for 94 feet when they're trying to bring the ball up the court."
> —Mateen Cleaves

The Spartans were most effective when running the floor and scoring easy baskets. Talent and a selfless attitude also helped.

On a few occasions, MSU bogged down in its half-court offense. That wouldn't happen as frequently if the press was on.

"When we went on big runs last year it was usually because of our tough defense and transition offense," said Morris Peterson, who scored 15 points against AIA. "I think if we pressed more, that could be a lot of fun."

It would also help keep the 10 players who Spartans coach Tom Izzo plans to use happier.

Pressing could make Izzo's substitution decisions easier. Much easier.

Players will get tired and welcome a breather. Subs coming in will play hard, knowing their time is short.

"We definitely have enough talent and enough players to do it," said Thomas Kelley, who collected eight points and eight assists in the exhibition. "Everybody on this team can run, from the point guards to the centers."

Pressing would make the most of the Spartans' talent.

Guards Mateen Cleaves, Kelley, Charlie Bell and Doug Davis are capable of running the court for 40 minutes. They are all effective defenders and unselfish on offense.

At small forward, Peterson and Jason Klein are gliders, who have improved defensively and are developing consistent outside shots.

MSU's big men can run too.

Antonio Smith is known as a bruiser, but he looks more like a basketball player and less like a football tight end. Andre Hutson, A.J. Granger and Adam Ballinger can execute a full-court press.

No team, not even early-season challengers Temple, Connecticut and Duke, enjoys facing a press.

What's In a Number?

Former Spartan Scott Skiles had his No. 4 jersey retired at Friday's season opener against Northeast Louisiana. Skiles, an All-America selection as a senior, also wore No. 25 for one season. The Spartans knocked off Northeast Louisiana 89-58 at the Breslin Center.

The Big Ten is stacked with quality guards. But those playmakers and 3-point specialists are less effective if they're holding their shorts trying to catch a breather as a result of the press.

"We could really wear down teams if we pressed," said Cleaves, who had 11 assists and eight points. "And I know point guards would hate to have a guy in their face for 94 feet when they're trying to bring the ball up the court."

MSU's weakness defensively is guarding talented centers. But if MSU is forcing teams to run, they won't be able to set up down low in a half-court offense.

What does Izzo think?

"I think you'll see us do more pressing than we have in the past," he said. "I don't think we'll get to a point to where we do it for an entire game, but I'll be surprised if we don't do it at all."

The strategy could pay dividends in the early going with road tests against the No. 7 Owls in Philadelphia (November 20) and against the No. 2 Huskies on December 5 in Storrs, Connecticut.

And it could bedevil top-ranked Duke, the Spartans' opponent at the Great Eight Tournament in Chicago on December 2.

After all, the 1998-99 Spartans are planning on making a run to the Final Four.

Why not get off to a fast start?

Open Sesame

Including Friday's victory against Northeast Louisiana, the Spartans have won 22 straight season openers. MSU's last season-opening loss came on November 29, 1976 when the Spartans dropped an 81-76 decision to Central Michigan in Mount Pleasant. The last time MSU dropped its home-opener came in the same season, when Western Michigan scored a 74-73 victory in the second game of the season.

Road to the Final Four

Non-Conference Games

Former MSU basketball great Scott Skiles had his number retired at halftime of the Spartans' 89-58 win over Northeast Louisiana.

MSU's Andre Hutson slams home a basket against Northeast Louisiana's Todd Daniels.

MSU's Mateen Cleaves passes to a teammate over Northeast Louisiana's seven-footer Wojciech Myrda.

Road to the Final Four

Non-Conference Games

MSU LETS BIG ONE GET AWAY

TEMPLE 60, MSU 59

NOVEMBER 21, 1998
JACK EBLING

PHILADELPHIA—It's a looooong season. And it was almost as long a game.

A split second too long for the Michigan State Spartans.

Dominating Temple, the favorite, for almost 38 minutes wasn't enough Friday night.

Not when a great effort was squandered with mental and physical errors.

As the hosts' fans flooded the floor, the only numbers that mattered were the ones on the scoreboard—60-59.

What matters more this morning is how Tom Izzo's team responds from the toughest loss in any of his players' careers.

"Leading by nine with 2 minutes left, I thought the only way we could lose was if we really screwed it up," said MSU forward Jason Klein.

That's one explanation for the Spartans' collapse—a finish we've seen all-too-often on the football field.

But the Owls deserve some credit, too, despite being outshot from the field 56.1 percent to 35.8.

Their trapping defense produced a string of five tie-ups and 15 second-half turnovers.

And after just 4-for-11 success from the foul line after the break, Temple hit the shots it had to have, as point guard Pepe Sanchez made five in a row to tie and to win with a half-second remaining.

Sanchez owned the last five minutes, outplaying All-American Mateen Cleaves.

In the clutch, a player who made all the right plays so often last season couldn't do anything right.

"This loss was my fault," said Cleaves, who had nine of his turnovers in the second half and missed a free throw with 52 seconds to play. "It was my kind of game . . . . I should've taken over at the end."

Amid the expected sniffles, Cleaves and co-captain Antonio Smith searched for answers in the one quiet room at The Apollo of Temple.

> **"With all the buildup I've had, it's up to me to win these games," Cleaves said.**

A sudden lack of aggression was probably as much to blame as anything—or anyone.

"We just couldn't be as aggressive as we wanted," said Smith of the Spartans' 27 fouls. "It was just their night. But our margin of error just isn't that great against good teams.

The seventh-ranked Owls were four-point favorites over a team that was ranked fourth in the USA TODAY/ESPN poll and fifth in the Associated Press poll.

And after falling behind by 15 points early in the second half, it looked as if MSU might toss John Chaney's team into the Delaware River.

Suddenly, the Spartans stopped attacking and pulled the ball back on what should have been a lob for Morris Peterson.

Before long, Temple took over and got the ball three times in the final minutes on a new tie-up rule that would have meant alternating possession last season.

"We let them take the fight to us in the last few minutes," Peterson said. "They applied a lot of pressure at the end. And we didn't react very well."

With former MSU basketball greats Julius McCoy, Sam Vincent and Eric Snow looking on, the clock seemed to tick in slow motion.

And after being abused by Cleaves for more than 30 minutes, Sanchez got his revenge by scoring nine of his 11 points in the last 2:07.

"We didn't suck it up in the last two minutes," Klein said in disbelief. "That's not how Michigan State plays."

It's certainly not how it wins on the road.

"With all the buildup I've had, it's up to me to win these games," Cleaves said. "We didn't relax with the lead at the end. We knew it would be a dogfight."

Neither team was a dog.

And both should be fighting in similar games in March, when a loss is a lot bigger letdown.

It's up to the Spartans to make sure they're celebrating after the next dramatic finish.

If they do, they can look to the lessons of a devastating loss with one consolation.

Defeats in November are never fatal.

They only feel that way.

Michigan State's Non-Conference Schedule And Results

Northeast Louisiana	W	89-58*
Oakland	W	96-66
Temple	L	60-59
Central Florida	W	87-64*
Western Michigan	W	90-66*
Duke	L	73-67
UConn	L	82-68
E. Tenn State	W	86-53
UI-Chicago	W	77-33*
Pepperdine	W	79-67
Tulsa	W	68-58
Alabama	W	75-58
UNC-Asheville	W	64-39*
Louisville	W	69-57*
MSU Non-Conference Record		11-3

*MSU home game

Road to the Final Four

Non-Conference Games

SPARTANS FALL WITH CHARACTER

DUKE 73, MSU 67

DECEMBER 3, 1998
JACK EBLING

CHICAGO—It was a very late start. And a very quick finish.

Over almost before it began.

But someone forgot to tell Michigan State the game was done when it trailed Duke 13-0 Wednesday.

Or 17-2.

Or 21-4.

When the night was through, there were two winners in the United Center.

The Blue Devils prevailed on the scoreboard 73-67 in the final game of the Great Eight.

And MSU won the respect of everyone who appreciates resiliency in college basketball.

It was the exact opposite of a 60-59 loss to Temple on November 20, when MSU blew a nine-point lead in the final 2:07.

This time, we were reminded of one of the game's great truths.

You can't lose a lead you never have.

Tom Izzo's team trailed for all but the game's first 32 seconds.

It spotted perhaps the nation's most talented team a 17-point edge in the first 7:49.

Then, the Spartans began a comeback that left them feeling totally frustrated.

If they needed a measuring stick for a still-maturing program, they got one here in the opening minutes.

Right between the eyes.

You can't spot a team a double-digit lead and expect to win, especially against the most successful team in the nation over a span of 14 years.

If Duke is what MSU hopes to be, it learned several things in its second loss to the Devils in the last five years.

The level of play required at the top means concentration and consistency for 40 minutes.

No team starts with a huge lead unless you let them.

And the gap is steadily shrinking between MSU and the sport's elite.

"We're getting to be a real good team for 30 minutes," Izzo said. "We played 35 minutes of good basketball at the beginning at Temple and 30 good minutes at the end tonight."

For what it's worth, Duke coach Mike Krzyzewski said the Spartans were as good an offensive rebounding team as his program has ever faced.

Izzo's team clawed within six at 36-30 with 39 seconds left in the half and got within five several times in the second half, and for an instant, were within three at 58-55.

For that, the Spartans should all thank forward Morris Peterson, the best player on the floor and a member of the All-Great Eight team.

Peterson was a pleasant surprise to the NBA scouts who crashed press row for lack of anything better to do.

It would have been hard for them to see anything better than the show Peterson and Duke's Trajan Langdon delivered, especially in the first half.

But in the end, the Devils were a little too big, a little too experienced and a little too lucky before a crowd of 19,412.

It was 54-47 when MSU power forward Antonio Smith scored on a drive and could have been fouled. Instead, the officials called a charge and waved off the basket.

Suddenly, what could have been a four-point game was a nine-point lead after a Duke basket.

It could have been four again when MSU point guard Mateen Cleaves had a basket waved off and didn't shoot a free throw he would have had if a non-shooting foul wasn't called.

And it didn't help that Cleaves was 3-for-17 from the field and outscored 14-8 by the Devils' William Avery.

"I'm not playing Mateen Cleaves basketball right now," he said in the understatement of the year. "I'm going to at some time. And when I do, we're going to be an awfully tough team to beat."

MSU Overcomes Barrage; Wins Spartan Classic

By David Birkett
November 29, 1998

EAST LANSING—Thankfully, the goal was to win a championship, not a 3-point contest.

No. 7 Michigan State survived dead-eye 3-point shooting by Kylo Jones to beat Western Michigan 90-66 in the Spartan Classic championship game Saturday night at a sold-out Breslin Center.

"Kylo Jones played fabulous. He really played well in a lot of ways."

Jones tied an MSU opponent record with eight 3-pointers. He scored a career-high 28 points, 22 in the first half, and finished 8-of-13 from 3-point range.

Tournament MVP Morris Peterson didn't miss much either. He scored a career-high 21 points on 8-of-12 shooting off the bench for Michigan State.

"Coach made it a point to run a little more," Peterson said. "We tried to get out on the break and do some things in the transition game. It started into us getting some easy baskets, those are types of things we're good at." The Spartans faced their biggest deficit of the season—nine points—midway through the half and didn't take their first lead of the game until 13:25 had elapsed.

Jones made his final 3-pointer of the half with 2:10 left, but the Spartans closed the period with six straight points to take a 40-35 lead.

After allowing 18 unanswered points in the first half, MSU held Jones in check much of the second half. He converted just two second-half 3-point tries after making 6-of-8 in the first stanza.

The Spartans embarked on a 10-0 run early in the second half to take a 60-50 lead. Jones cut the Broncos' deficit to seven with a 3-pointer, but WMU never got any closer. MSU closed the game with a 22-6 run.

Road to the Final Four

Non-Conference Games

Michigan State's Mateen Cleaves (12) goes up with a shot over Duke's Shane Battier (31) as Michigan State's Andre Hutson awaits a possible rebound.

MSU's Andre Huston looks for a shot under the basket as WMU's Emil Mulic tries to block.

Road to the Final Four

Non-Conference Games

UCONN EXPOSES SPARTANS

UConn 82, MSU 68

DECEMBER 6, 1998
JACK EBLING

STORRS—There was no woulda, coulda, shoulda this time. No. 9 Michigan State was spanked in the second half Saturday at Connecticut and beaten by a better college basketball team.

An 82-68 final doesn't reflect a 19-point margin with 55 seconds left.

It doesn't describe the top-ranked Huskies' dominance inside and out.

And it doesn't reveal the level of MSU's frustration and bewilderment after the game.

At 4-3 overall, the Spartans have precisely the record I predicted they would at this juncture.

But they have several more problems than they should with all but one contributor back from a Big Ten co-champion and NCAA Sweet 16 team.

Tom Izzo's players won't win their last seven non-conference games and rule the league, as almost everyone expects, unless at least three things occur:

Point guard Mateen Cleaves must play significantly better at both ends of the court.

He has to have more support, especially from backup Thomas Kelley, who has been only slightly better than he was when he sat out all last season.

> "You've got to have character when you go on the road," Smith said. "When you play in the NCAA Tournament, you're going to have to play back-to-back games against tough teams. We'd better get used to it."

And MSU must find the attitude it had last year when it was one of the nation's hungriest teams and biggest surprises.

Especially in hostile environments like Gampel Pavilion, where the UConn students camped out for seats, then stood and roared the entire game.

After responding to guest announcer Michael Buffer's cry of "LET'S GET READY TO ROUND-BALLLLLL" by grabbing a quick 11-2 lead, the Spartans were caught and passed in a more-than-respectable 38-34 first half.

That was close as they ever got, as Cleaves was 2-for-15 from the field and was outscored 20-6 by UConn's squatty Khalid El-Amin.

Counting the work of Kelley, Charlie Bell and Doug Davis, MSU's backcourt was a combined 6-for-32 from the field, while a frontcourt led by Morris Peterson, Andre Hutson and Antonio Smith went 25-for-38.

"Our effort in the second half wasn't what Michigan State basketball is," Peterson said. "We had our chances early. . . . I can't explain it. We got outhustled and outefforted."

Outpassed, outshot and outdefended, too.

But it was the lack of sustained intensity that was most troubling.

With a shot at their first win over a No. 1-ranked team since the 1979 NCAA Championship, the Spartans lost more than a game.

As the UConn students shouted "O-VER-RA-TED!" at every opportunity in the second half, MSU squandered a great opportunity to shut them up.

"You've got to have character when you go on the road," Smith said. "When you play in the NCAA Tournament, you're going to have to play back-to-back games against tough teams. We'd better get used to it."

So much for the excuse that the Spartans got tired after their game with Duke late Wednesday night and a 4:30 a.m. arrival in Lansing on Thursday morning.

If they were tired of anything, it was of the feeling they've had in three losses this season.

"If guys aren't getting tired of losing, they've got to start getting tired of it," Hutson said. "We haven't played a complete game yet. To become a championship team, we have to do that."

To become a very good one, it's just as important.

And to do that, it'll take leadership from Cleaves—in a positive direction.

"They took the fight to us after awhile," Bell said. "We showed we could run with them early on. But they regrouped. I guess they wanted it more than we did."

If that's the case, it's something Izzo will work to change.

Even before he deals with Cleaves' jump shot.

MSU's Jason Klein battles UConn All-American Richard Hamilton.

Road to the Final Four

Non-Conference Games

CLEAVES SEEKS TOUCH

DECEMBER 6, 1998
LARRY LAGE

STORRS—Mateen Cleaves' swagger and smiles have vanished. So has his jump shot.

Michigan State's star guard thrives on emotion, but when you can't seem to make a basket, it's tough to pound your chest or beam with confidence.

Cleaves missed 13-of-15 shots in the No. 9 Spartans' 82-68 loss to top-ranked Connecticut on Saturday in Gampel Pavilion.

The lackluster performance comes just three days after he missed 14-of-17 shots in a 73-67 loss to No. 4 Duke in Chicago.

The consensus preseason All-American finished with six points, seven assists, one turnover and two rebounds.

How does Cleaves plan to break out of his funk?

"I'm going to shoot with my eyes closed," the frustrated Cleaves said.

"I missed the whole summer, that's what hurts."

Cleaves was unable to practice for more than two months because of ankle and shoulder injuries.

CBS analyst Billy Packer said that's the root of the problem.

"His shot was the No. 1 thing he needed to work on last summer, but he couldn't due to his injuries," Packer said. "He's clearly not playing with the confidence that he used to have."

That was obvious on several occasions Saturday, but never more so than in one sequence with less than seven minutes left in the first half.

Cleaves was standing by himself about 15 feet from the basket. After thinking about shooting, he chose to dribble away.

Seconds later, he tossed the ball to Antonio Smith in the same spot he just vacated. The power forward took and made the basket without hesitation.

Cleaves didn't get many open looks at the basket, thanks to an outstanding defensive effort from the Huskies' Ricky Moore.

"I get excited when I'm going to guard one of the best point guards in the country," Moore said. "That's what I live for."

Izzo said he was happy with how controlled Cleaves played in the first half. Cleaves had four assists and one turnover while missing 4-of-5 shots.

"Mateen Cleaves played like the player we had last year in the first half," Izzo said.

In the second half, Cleaves tried and failed to create shots off the dribble near the basket and with 3-point attempts.

"I think Mateen got frustrated in the second half," Izzo said. "Partly with himself and partly because some of our guys that had been playing well had awful games."

Cleaves did not dodge the media after the game, but was uncharacteristically short and expressionless in the locker room after the game.

"It's hard because I want to win and have fun," Cleaves said. "But sometimes, God works in mysterious ways. Things don't always go your way, but you have to suck it up and work through it."

It's fitting that MSU's Jason Klein scores by "driving" on a famous North Carolina name in the Spartans' 64-39 non-conference victory against UNC-Asheville.

Road to the Final Four

Non-Conference Games

MSU 79, Pepperdine 67

"MO P." DELIVERS AGAIN

DECEMBER 22, 1998
JACK EBLING

LAIE, Hawaii—He ought to have a nickname. That's what Pepperdine coach Lorenzo Romar suggested. But "Mo P." isn't sufficient for a player like Michigan State all-purpose star Morris Peterson.

That tag he has carried since his earliest days on the playgrounds of Flint can't do him justice.

"Sweet Pete" would be considerably better.

So would "Mo-Mentum."

Without his help in every phase of the game, the Spartans wouldn't have beaten the Waves 79-67 Monday in the first game of the first Pearl Harbor Classic.

They wouldn't be 7-3 this morning.

And they wouldn't be able to play with a team like 10-1 Tulsa, tonight's semifinal opponent.

Tom Izzo's players might not be able to withstand the force of the Golden Hurricane with Peterson's presence.

Without him, they could forget about winning a tournament title—and defending a share of the Big Ten championship when they get home and have to wear jackets again.

In MSU's first win by less than 23 points this season, it was Peterson who turned a serious scare into a satisfying score.

"He scores points pretty easily, doesn't he?" Romar said. "You can give him a nickname—something other than 'The Microwave.' But it should probably be something like that."

It should be something that shows the improvement a 6-foot-6 junior has made in the past 12 months—as great a leap as any Spartan has had since Scott Skiles raised his game to another level as a senior in 1985-86.

After averaging 8.0 points and 3.5 rebounds as a redshirt-sophomore, Peterson has raised those totals to 14.5 points per game, the most of any MSU player, and 5.5 rebounds, second behind fellow "Flintstone" Antonio Smith.

"He's a lot more mature," Smith said. "His head is in the game more. He always had that kind of potential. But wearing that cast last year probably helped him."

> "Coach (Tom) Crean always tells me if I get the defense going, everything else takes care of itself," Peterson said. "It's just a matter of being hungry. And I'm really hungry to win this year."

Peterson credits his work in the Flint Pro-Am Summer League and a new dedication to defense, with or without "The Club" he wore last year to protect a broken left wrist.

If he played 35 minutes a game instead of his average of 23.8, his numbers might really be eye-popping, since he has boosted his field goal percentage from 44.5 to an even 60.

For now, he's happy to come off the bench as a backup to Jason Klein.

And MSU coach Tom Izzo is content to keep Peterson in that limited-but-essential role.

"It's tempting," Izzo said. "I discuss that with the staff nearly every night. I'll have to start asking my wife, I guess. But he can go in and help us in so many different areas. He can play the three (small forward), the two (shooting guard), the four (power forward) and even check a point guard."

Peterson put the clamps on Pepperdine standout Jelani Gardner, a 6-6 point guard, and still had game-highs of 18 points and seven rebounds in 29 minutes.

He handled the ball against pressure and beat the Waves down the floor in transition, while diving for more loose balls than he used to go for in entire months as a freshman.

"He's playing so much harder," Cleaves said. "He always had tools, back when we played in elementary school. But he put it on himself to do a lot of extra shooting. And he has realized that everyone feeds off his defense."

The Spartans have been eating well, with Peterson—not Cleaves, a returning All-American—as their meal ticket.

"Coach (Tom) Crean always tells me if I get the defense going, everything else takes care of itself," Peterson said. "It's just a matter of being hungry. And I'm really hungry to win this year."

Maybe that's the name he needs.

"Mo-Tivated."

MSU Tops Alabama for Title

By Jack Ebling
December 24, 1998

LAIE, Hawaii—Michigan State earned its second tournament title this season with a 75-58 win over Alabama on Wednesday night in the inaugural Pearl Harbor Classic.

Forward A.J. Granger was the key performer with 16 points, six more than his previous best, while point guard Mateen Cleaves had a team-high 17 and forward Morris Peterson, the tourney MVP, added 12.

"You've got to take your hat off to the kid," MSU coach Tom Izzo said of Granger, who missed the day's preparation because his father, Joe, suffered a serious neck injury in a bodysurfing accident. "That just shows coaching means nothing. It was the best game of his career for sure."

Alabama scored the first seven points of the second half to grab a 43-37 lead. But Granger hit a huge 3-pointer. And the Spartans went back in front on putbacks by guard Charlie Bell and Peterson.

It was 45-all when Cleaves hit a 3 from the top of the key and Granger connected from 12 and 21 feet for a 53-47 lead.

A pair of free throws by Granger and a fast-break layup by Kelley made it a 10-point game. And Alabama never drew closer than six, as Cleaves and forwards Andre Hutson and Antonio Smith answered with five slick offensive plays.

Road to the Final Four

Non-Conference Games

MSU 69, LOUISVILLE 57

SPARTANS REFUSE TO SPUTTER

JANUARY 3, 1999
JACK EBLING

EAST LANSING—The sleepwalkers who wore Michigan State uniforms Wednesday night didn't all transfer.

They just woke up to a basketball alarm and were alert enough to beat Louisville Saturday.

In an eye-opening performance, the Spartans looked more like last winter's warriors in their 11th double-digit victory this season.

Before a CBS national audience and an estimated 8,000 "honorary Yoopers," MSU grabbed a 10-0 advantage and never trailed in a 69-57 triumph over a team that handled Kentucky last weekend.

With plenty of praise to distribute, let's start with Tom Izzo and his coaching staff.

Instead of accepting a 25-point walkthrough against UNC-Asheville, Izzo realized a similar effort might lead to an opposite massacre.

The iron-willed Iron Mountain man ripped his players as much as he ever has after a win and shook up a lineup that seemed a bit stagnant.

But no one deserves more credit than the four players who switched assignments—new starters Morris Peterson and A.J. Granger and substitutes Charlie Bell and Andre Hutson.

> "I tried to go down near the end of the bench," Bell said. "They told me, 'What are you doing? ... Get outta here!' They have some kind of thing down there. So I wound up back by the coaches."

"I told Charlie to sit back and watch what was happening," said Peterson, the best player on the court in almost every Spartan game this season. "I thought he did a great job when it was his turn to play."

If Izzo is right when he says his team has eight legitimate starters, he had to be as happy with the attitudes as the results on the floor.

Or as thrilled as any admitted perfectionist can be.

"I'm not sure," Izzo said, when asked if the switches jump-started some batteries. "Morris had 23 points today. And he had 23 off the bench. So he's versatile. He's able to do it both ways."

Bell and Hutson were able to check their egos at the entrance of the Breslin Center and answer their critics with nine and eight rebounds, respectively—the game's two highest totals.

Hutson added seven points, all at the foul line, and was a key factor despite second-half foul trouble and zero field goal attempts.

Former MSU All-American Steve Smith holds his framed Spartan jersey Saturday at the Breslin Center during ceremonies where Smith's number was officially retired.

"I wasn't playing as hard as I should have been," Hutson said. "And that's the way Coach should have reacted. With the guys we have, if someone isn't playing well, he should be replaced."

Depth can be as important in practice as it ever is in a game, which pushes everyone to compete and prepare even harder.

For Bell, who had started all 43 games in his college career, the biggest challenge was to figure out where to sit when the game began.

"I tried to go down near the end of the bench," Bell said. "They told me, 'What are you doing? ... Get outta here!' They have some kind of thing down there. So I wound up back by the coaches."

Bell's six offensive rebounds were as important as any statistic. And he had the presence of mind to poke fun at a teammate.

"When I missed a shot and got it back, I was just doing what Antonio Smith does and padding my rebound stats," he said. "Actually, I just wanted to play hard. Coach said he wanted to try something new. I was for doing that, too."

If he hadn't been, Smith and Mateen Cleaves would have administered a little attitude adjustment physically and verbally.

Smith might have put Bell or Hutson in a headlock.

Cleaves would just have reminded either one what it means to be part of a winner.

"Charlie showed a lot of character today," Cleaves said. "He came out and played and sucked up his pride. It was the same with Andre. He could have been down in the dumps. But that's not what this team is about."

It's about ready to climb back into the Top 10, whether the pollsters see that or not.

At 11-3, with seven straight wins and momentum heading into the Big Ten season, it isn't who starts that matters.

Not for a team that's just getting started.

Road to the Final Four

Big Ten Season

WISCONSIN 66, MSU 51

SPARTANS GET LESSON ON ROAD

JANUARY 7, 1999
JACK EBLING

MADISON—Less than 10 months ago, the Michigan State Spartans won a share of the Big Ten basketball title at the Kohl Center.

Wednesday night, they stood and watched the Wisconsin Badgers win something else here.

Their self-esteem.

The Spartans did everything a visitor could to put the Badgers back among the living in a 66-51 shocker.

And if they don't play any better against Michigan, a team that beat Wisconsin 59-55 in Ann Arbor, they might be as desperate as the Badgers were after an 0-2 Big Ten start.

Falling behind 9-0 on the road and failing to score for the first 7:13 was hardly the plan Tom Izzo designed.

Passing up a dozen good shots and turning 12 more good looks into tough ones isn't usually the way to win.

But MSU battled back and led 27-24 at halftime, thanks in part to the Badger fans.

Spartan guard Mateen Cleaves was 0-for-3 from the field in a pointless first 18:39 when he stepped to the foul line and heard chants of "AL-CO-HOL-IC!"

Cleaves promptly hit two free throws, then ended the half with penetration and a left-handed bank.

But Wisconsin was just getting started, as a 15-6 run in the first 5:06 of the second half re-energized a sleepy crowd.

> The Spartans did everything a visitor could to put the Badgers back among the living in a 66-51 shocker.

Big Ten Season

20

Or maybe it just seemed silent compared to the "Traveling Izzone," 100 members of MSU's student section, who bused to Madison and had a great time for a while.

But all the chants in the world can't will a ball into the basket.

Especially when the Spartans had no clue where it was.

Yes, they made their first 16 free throws before guard Thomas Kelley missed the front end of a one-and-one opportunity.

The trouble was they also missed their first 14 shots from 3-point range and were completely dominated in the last 20 minutes.

By then, the chant for a 12th-ranked team had changed to "O-VER-RA-TED!"

"I thought we were playing terrible in the first half and were lucky to be where we were," said forward Jason Klein. "I thought if we picked it up a little bit, we'd be all right."

Instead, they had to pick up their jaws as the hosts produced a 42-24 advantage the rest of the way.

Cleaves was terrible at times and threw up airballs from makeable distances.

A loss at Wisconsin to open the Spartans' Big Ten season was not the direction that coach Tom Izzo had pointed for his team.

And Klein was as cold as the sub-zero temperatures on nearby Lake Mendota.

MSU is a fairly deep team—one of the deeper squads in the league.

But when nearly everyone has frostbite, even the deepest team is in deep trouble.

Road to the Final Four

Big Ten Season

SPARTANS SHAKE FUNK, STOP U-M

MSU 81, MICHIGAN 67

JANUARY 10, 1999
LARRY LAGE

EAST LANSING—Michigan State picked a good time to break out of its uptight shell.

The 12th-ranked Spartans smiled, danced and celebrated during their 81-67 win over Michigan on Saturday in front of 14,659 at the Breslin Center on a day that the 1979 national championship team was honored.

"We just went out, had fun and relaxed," MSU senior forward Antonio Smith said. "That was the biggest key."

Mateen Cleaves' play didn't hurt.

The junior point guard led the Spartans with 25 points (on 7-of-10 shooting), eight assists and four steals.

"Mateen was good today," Michigan coach Brian Ellerbe said. "He got some really good looks and knocked down his shots. He was a big factor."

Morris Peterson complemented Cleaves with 16 points.

Jason Klein had 12 points and six rebounds. Antonio Smith scored 10 points and grabbed a game-high eight rebounds.

"We were having fun again, maybe for the first time since last year," said Klein, who had a game-high four offensive rebounds. "Magic (Johnson) told us before the game that fun leads to wins and wins lead to championships.

"We're going to try and follow his advice."

MSU did an exceptional job of shutting down Michigan's two star guards—Louis Bullock and Robbie Reid.

Bullock, who was averaging 21.5 points, scored just six points in the first 35 minutes of the game and finished with 15 on 3-of-14 shooting.

Reid, who was averaging 12.6 points, had seven points on 2-of-8 shooting.

Josh Asselin led Michigan with a career-high 17 points.

MSU entered the season with high expectations—internally and from its fans.

The Spartans responded by playing methodical basketball without much emotion.

Four losses to ranked teams followed while some started to question whether the Spartans deserved to be mentioned among the nation's elite teams.

Shooters lost their instinct to shoot.

> "We were having fun again, maybe for the first time since last year," said Klein.

Rebounders forgot how to crash the boards. Defensive players started to get beat.

The Spartans met with and without coaches several times after a loss to Wisconsin earlier in the week to discuss the situation.

"When we watched film of our games you could tell we weren't having fun any more," MSU guard Charlie Bell said. "We decided we had to start having fun again and playing our roles.

"And it especially hit home when Magic told us to stop playing too tight and just relax. That's what we did today."

Another key for the Spartans was how they finished the first half.

MSU led the entire game, but U-M cut the deficit to one on four occasions in the first half.

The last time it happened, with 2:56 left, the Spartans responded with a 10-0 run to take a 38-27 halftime lead.

"That was crucial," Ellerbe said. "We can't have those type of runs affect us. But we let it happen and that's a tough thing to swallow."

The Wolverines opened the second half by outscoring the Spartans 7-2, which cut MSU's lead to 40-34 with 16:58 left.

MSU bumped its lead back to double digits. The victory was sealed with a stingy stretch of defense.

Michigan did not make a field goal for more than seven minutes after Peter Vignier made a layup at the 12:32 mark.

MSU coach Tom Izzo didn't want to describe his team's demeanor as loose, but he was happy to see the Spartans smiling, hugging and winning convincingly.

Former Spartan coaches, players and managers gather at center court to celebrate 100 years of MSU basketball.

Road to the Final Four

Big Ten Season

COLLEGE GAME IS FANTASTIC

MSU 71, MINNESOTA 55

JANUARY 14, 1999
JACK EBLING

EAST LANSING—Do basketball fans really love that game?

Or just that guy?

We're about to find out.

With the NBA back in business, we'll learn how long it takes to forgive.

And with His Airness now a spectator, we'll see if it's possible to forget.

Eventually, the crowds will return.

Michael Jordan won't.

Even if he did, there's a better alternative.

The college game.

If you saw Michigan State whip Minnesota 71-55 Wednesday night, you know the reasons.

There was more sweat expended in the first half than in any pro game before the NBA playoffs.

There was more team basketball—sorry, two-man games with one pick-and-roll play don't count—than in a week of TNT and TBS telecasts.

And there was more passion in the stands than you'd have with kissing contests in 10 sections of The Palace.

The execution was far from perfect.

But when hasn't it been?

Game 6 of the NBA Finals last year?

> As good players come and great ones go after years of noticeable growth, the names on the front of the uniforms never change. Only the coaches' blood pressure does.

Not when Jordan finished 15-for-35 from the field and Utah fell to Chicago in the final minute with sloppy ballhandling and slipping defense.

It's the last steal and shot we remember.

The big plays and the big players.

Wednesday, we saw plenty of both.

MSU couldn't protect a 28-14 lead and let the Golden Gophers back in the game.

Just when Minnesota was set to draw even, the Spartans answered with back-to-back-to-back 3-pointers by little-used point guard Lorenzo Guess, acrobatic forward Morris Peterson and acting center A.J. Granger.

Seconds later, Granger drew a charge with no acting involved and gave up his body—his head, too—without worrying about incentive clauses.

Earlier, Peterson had a breakaway slam on a fast-break pass from quarterback Mateen Cleaves that brought everyone, not just The Izzone, out of their seats.

But that was nothing compared to the noise three times in the second half when the better team got its bearings and pulled away.

That's partly because the teams are what counts in college ball, not some $120 million man.

As good players come and great ones go after years of noticeable growth, the names on the front of the uniforms never change.

Only the coaches' blood pressure does.

MSU hit just 36.4 percent from the field and 33.3 at the line in the first half and more than made up for that lack of precision with intensity at both ends of the court.

And with a huge game from forward Jason Klein.

After scoring just four points in a loss at Wisconsin last week, he answered his doubters with 12 points against Michigan and 21 against Minnesota.

Klein should have had three more if not for surprising misses at the foul line.

But he was 4-for-7 from 3-point range—just what Tom Izzo wanted.

And needed with the presence of 7-foot-1 shot-eater Joel Przybilla, a freshman who could be downright scary in seasons to come.

He finished with eight blocked shots, four times as many as the winners.

Przybilla didn't alter the outcome but was as entertaining as halftime dance puppeteer Christopher and the timeout breaks with the MSU Motion.

Those performers had almost as much energy as the Spartans showed on the boards, with 18 offensive rebounds to just one for the Gophers.

They won the game and kept the fans' hearts by hitting the floor for every loose ball.

There was no Jordan on either team—just guys who played as hard.

MSU's Mateen Cleaves looks to pass to teammate Charlie Bell after grabbing a loose ball in the Spartans' 71-55 victory over Minnesota.

Road to the Final Four

Big Ten Season

SPARTANS SLIP PAST ILLINOIS

MSU 51, ILLINOIS 49

JANUARY 17, 1999
LARRY LAGE

CHAMPAIGN—Big Ten favorite Michigan State narrowly escaped a major upset Saturday night, edging lightly regarded Illinois 51-49 in Assembly Hall.

The Spartans, ranked 10th in the USA TODAY/ESPN poll, 14th by The Associated Press, didn't catch their breath until a 50-foot shot by Illinois' Cory Bradford at the buzzer bounced off the back of the rim.

Fortunately for MSU, Morris Peterson was able to catch and convert alley-oop passes from Mateen Cleaves.

Cleaves and Peterson's third high-wire hookup gave the Spartans a 49-45 lead with the shot clock winding down and 18.4 seconds left to play.

"We were trying to get a shot for Jason (Klein), but the play broke down," Cleaves said. "I saw Pete flying down the baseline so I just threw it up to him and let him go get it."

Coach Tom Izzo credited the Illini for giving his team trouble with their zone defense. But he wasn't thrilled that MSU's top option against the zone was the alley-oop.

"It's kind of sad when that play is your best play," Izzo said.

Bradford made the score 49-47 on a jumper with 10.3 seconds left. MSU's Andre Hutson then made two free throws .7 seconds later to push the lead back to four.

Bradford's 19-footer with three seconds left sliced the lead to 51-49.

MSU's Antonio Smith then missed the front end of a one-and-one, giving Bradford and the Illini their final desperation chance.

The Spartans' aggressive play and blow-out victory at home against the Illini were in sharp contrast with their narrow escape from Champaign in January.

Road to the Final Four

Big Ten Season

SPARTANS SERVE NOTICE

MSU 80, IOWA 65

JANUARY 22, 1999
JACK EBLING

EAST LANSING—The idea is to put the ball in the hole. Not to climb into one. Once Michigan State remembered that Thursday night, the battle for first place in the Big Ten was little more than a scrimmage.

Anyone who didn't see the game could be misled by the final score.

An 80-65 win over Iowa was three games in one.

But the second subplot lasted the longest and was by far the most revealing.

After digging a 19-4 crater, the Spartans delivered a 19-minute stretch of excellence that won't soon be forgotten.

MSU went from 15 down to 20 up with a 43-8 surge.

And if it's much too soon to say which team will win the conference title, there's no doubt about the No. 1 program in the league today.

The same players who forgot to show up last Saturday night in Champaign, Illinois, arrived in time to erase one of the scariest starts in Breslin Center history.

When the Spartans realized who and where they were with 12:27 left in the first half, a delirious, disbelieving crowd and an ESPN audience saw the makings of a Final Four team.

The final 13:40 of the game was a desperate attempt by the Hawkeyes to stop the clock and steal the ball, with reasonable success.

But the better team won, as defending champions should in their buildings.

MSU answered every challenge to win at home and produce enough big plays to serve notice there might not be a tie at the top this time.

Eleven wins in the last 12 games have come in all shapes and sizes.

This one came with superior defense, solid shooting and better ballhandling than anyone envisioned.

The Spartans had 19 assists to Iowa's nine and just 14 turnovers to the Hawkeyes' 21.

That control of the ball and a surprising edge in 3-point shooting made all the difference.

As a result, MSU picked up its fourth win in five conference games and its 15th in 19 tries overall.

> **MSU answered every challenge to win at home and produce enough big plays to serve notice there might not be a tie at the top this time.**

Road to the Final Four...

Big Ten Season

SPARTANS HAMMER HOOSIERS

MSU 73, INDIANA 59

JANUARY 25, 1999
LARRY LAGE

BLOOMINGTON—Mateen Cleaves and Antonio Smith were sprawled out under Michigan State's basket like victims in a car crash.

But only two stretchers and an ambulance could've taken the Spartan duo out of Sunday's game in Assembly Hall.

Cleaves, Smith and the rest of the Spartans didn't want to miss Michigan State's biggest win of the season, a 73-59 victory over Indiana before 17,436 screaming Hoosier fans and a CBS national television audience.

The MSU victory, its fifth straight and 12th the last 13 games, was its first win in Bloomington since 1990.

The Spartans' effort nearly turned disastrous late in the second half when Cleaves and Smith collided under the Spartan basket. Both players stayed on the floor for a few moments in obvious pain.

But neither was going to stay down.

"Get up 'Mo,' we've got six minutes left," Smith said to Cleaves, ignoring the throbbing pain in his right ankle.

They limped off the court, but only sat on the bench for 31 seconds before re-entering the game to help the Spartans seal an impressive victory.

"Nothing would've stopped him and me from going back in," said Cleaves, who bruised his tailbone on the play with MSU ahead 61-50. "I didn't care if something was broken.

"We wanted to win this game more than anything in the world today."

The Spartans maintained sole possession of first place in the conference with their first win over a ranked opponent on the road.

MSU is now No. 8 in the latest USA TODAY/ESPN poll and will find out if it improved upon its 11th ranking in the Associated Press poll later today.

Cleaves led MSU with 16 points (on 6-of-12 shooting) and 13 assists, which tied the career-best mark he set in the win over Indiana last year in East Lansing.

Jason Klein and Morris Peterson added 13 each on a combined 12-of-20 shooting performance. A.J. Granger added 10 off the bench.

Indiana's A.J. Guyton scored 23 points and prevented the Hoosiers from being embarrassed in the first half with a scoring spree.

The junior guard scored 16 points in the final 6:46 of the half to help cut MSU's 30-14 lead to 36-34.

The Spartans led 38-34 at halftime.

"I said we had a run and they had a run," coach Tom Izzo said about his halftime talk to his team. "Then I said, 'Let's make sure the last run goes our way.'"

It did.

MSU went on an 11-0 run, capped by a Cleaves 3-pointer, midway through the second half. The burst gave the visitors command of the game with a 58-45 lead, with 8:40 left to play.

MSU's 11-0, second-half run was keyed by an impressive display of defense. The Spartans held Indiana without a point from the 16:00 mark until there was 7:54 left in the game and without a field goal for another 1:21.

The Spartans stymied the Hoosiers by switching from a man-to-man defense to a 3-2 zone, to help protect Peterson and Charlie Bell, who had four fouls each.

Indiana missed 12 straight shots and went 15 possessions without a field goal.

"I think we confused them with the zone," Klein said. "The coaches made a great decision to go with it."

The Hoosiers couldn't get closer than nine points in the final six minutes.

Luke Recker, who scored 52 points in his last two games, was 0-for-6 from the field and scored just one point from the line for Indiana.

Coach Bob Knight was not surprised at how well MSU played on his home court.

"I thought last year Michigan State would move up and be really, really good this year," Knight said. "The schedule they played early hurt them in terms of their record, but in the long run, it will really help them."

Indiana's Luke Jimenez, left, with Luke Recker, center, knocks the basketball away from MSU's Jason Klein (44) in the first half in Bloomington.

Road to the Final Four...

Big Ten Season

IZZO GIVES BACK

JANUARY 25, 1999
JACK EBLING

BLOOMINGTON—They had nothing to do with the victory Sunday. And everything to do with the type of winning program Michigan State wants.

The kind it has with Tom Izzo as head coach.

Seated at the end of the MSU bench for a 73-59 triumph at Indiana were John Cawood III, age 12, and his brother Anders, 10, of Okemos.

A few rows up and closer to midcourt were their uncle—Bill, a Spartan co-captain in 1982-83—and their grandpa Jack, class of '47.

Bill and Jack weren't in Assembly Hall because they're MSU's only father-son basketball lettermen.

They made the trip because Izzo wanted Johnny and Anders to be a part of the team.

Because he saw a great opportunity for both boys to bond with important male family members.

And because John Cawood Jr., a great friend and a better person, couldn't have been happier at the thought.

Unless he'd been alive to be with them.

When John was stricken with cancer last spring, when Becky and the boys went with him to Seattle for an unsuccessful bone marrow transplant and every day until a cerebral hemorrhage took his life last fall, he lived for so much more than himself.

He lived for the things he believed and the people he loved.

Izzo wasn't the first to see that.

But he and his wife, Lupe, were there to help in any way they could.

"John was a great guy," Izzo said before the trip began Saturday. "We wanted to do something to help the family. I just hope we can do that."

Before the game, a seventh-grade center for Chippewa Middle School talked about talks with the MSU coaches and words he won't forget from the players.

He'd been at Izzo's basketball camp enough to know how things were done.

So when the bus from the hotel to the shootaround left on time, one minute before the Cawoods reported, the only course of action was to grab a cab.

"We knocked until someone came to the door," Bill said. "I said that I was an assistant coach and

> And as you looked down the bench, the unforgettable image was of a conversation last winter, when John Jr. was the picture of health—and a gentle giant of a youth basketball coach.

Coach Tom Izzo and his wife, Lupe, shown here celebrating the Spartans' championship in the Big Ten Tournament, honored the memory of their friend John Cawood, Jr. by inviting John's two sons to join the Spartan bench for a key Big Ten battle against Indiana.

John was a player. When they let us in, John said, 'Uncle Bill, don't lie!'"

Johnny was just as concerned when his uncle told him, "Don't jump up too much or the officials can give you a bench technical."

But some games are impossible to sit through, especially when your younger brother nearly hit the score on the nose with a pregame prediction.

Today, they'll be back in school—the envy of every Spartan fan.

And for a family that has experienced so much pain, it's about time there was one of those days.

"What a wonderful, once-in-a-lifetime opportunity," Becky said from home before tipoff. "With Tom and Lupe, that doesn't surprise me. When I watched the plane take off, I had tears in my eyes."

It was something a lot of first-place coaches would never have considered.

But it was just what you'd expect of Izzo, who wants to build bridges and relationships the way Cawood Building Co. builds houses.

And as you looked down the bench, the unforgettable image was of a conversation last winter, when John Jr. was the picture of health—and a gentle giant of a youth basketball coach.

After Izzo had finished saying all the right things to a group of 11- and 12-year-olds in Breslin Center, he received an unsolicited tribute.

"I think Tom's more than the Coach of the Year," John said. "He's the Coach of the Next Generation. He's a builder of people."

He didn't live to see those words in Izzo's chapter of "Magic Moments: A Century of Spartan Basketball."

But chances are he saw his sons, his brother and his dad from a higher spot than any seat in Assembly Hall.

Road to the Final Four

Big Ten Season

MSU 76, OHIO STATE 71

SPARTANS COME BACK

JANUARY 28, 1999
LARRY LAGE

EAST LANSING—Michigan State beat Ohio State 76-71 Wednesday at the Breslin Center to remain on top of the conference and keep its win streak alive.

The Spartans have won six straight and 13 of their last 14 games.

Mateen Cleaves led his eighth-ranked team with 16 points and four consecutive free throws in the final 44.6 seconds to seal the win.

Jason Klein and Charlie Bell had 14 each. Morris Peterson scored 10 points.

Michael Redd led Ohio State with 20 points. Scoonie Penn added 17.

MSU stormed back from a 42-34 deficit with 14:36 left to take command of the game.

The Spartans went on a 22-7 run over the next eight minutes to take a 56-49 lead with 6:36 left. Six different players, led by Jason Klein's two 3-pointers, contributed offensively to help MSU during the burst.

> "In the first half we weren't into the game and the crowd wasn't in it," Klein said. "We needed that run to get us going and the crowd going."

"In the first half we weren't into the game and the crowd wasn't in it," Klein said. "We needed that run to get us going and the crowd going."

But the game was far from over.

Ohio State scored five straight points to cut its deficit to one.

MSU responded by outscoring the Buckeyes 10-4 to take a 66-59 lead with 1:45 remaining on a Charlie Bell dunk.

The Spartans' lead remained above five until a Neshaun Coleman 3-pointer made the score 70-66 with 37.5 seconds left.

After Cleaves made two free throws, Redd made a 3-pointer with nine seconds left to cut Ohio State's deficit to 72-69.

After Peterson connected on two free throws, Penn made two with 4.7 seconds left. Cleaves' final two free throws completed the Spartans' scoring.

Road to the Final Four

Big Ten Season

Much of the credit for Michigan State's success in crunch time has been attributed to the skill and hard work of Coach Tom Izzo, who earned National Coach of the Year honors in 1998.

MSU's Jason Klein battles for the rebound against Ohio State.

Road to the Final Four

Big Ten Season

SPARTANS SMOTHER NU STAR

MSU 65, NORTHWESTERN 48

JANUARY 31, 1999
JACK EBLING

EAST LANSING—If you listen to Northwestern coaches, Evan Eschmeyer is twice the player he was last season.

But if you look at his stats Saturday night against Michigan State, he had half the game he did last year against the Spartans.

That battle between college basketball's No. 1 big man and a battalion of defenders was the story behind a 65-48 mismatch.

The Spartans sped up the tempo and held Eschmeyer to 15 points on 3-for-9 shooting from the field—a stark contrast to his 30 points and 12-for-18 accuracy last January 31.

If the only player in the nation averaging more than 20 points and 10 rebounds ever has a tougher time, it'll be as an NBA rookie next year.

The 6-foot-11, 255-pounder was wrestled by MSU's Antonio Smith, A.J. Granger and Andre Hutson, while the MSU guards took turns swooping in to make life miserable.

For a sixth-year senior who missed two seasons with a nerve and bone condition in his foot, his last visit to Breslin Center—we think—was as much fun as another operation.

"The last time I saw that much contact was in a karate movie," Northwestern coach Kevin O'Neill said. "I'm tired of it. He's tired of it. And his mother's tired of it. . . . She told me to say that."

O'Neill's appreciation for the Spartans and his friendship with Tom Izzo told him to say something else—that MSU is by far the best team the Wildcats have played and a probable top-five team next week.

The Spartans' up-tempo play and swarming defense shut down Northwestern and Wildcat star Evan Eschmeyer.

Road to the Final Four

Big Ten Season

Big Ten Conference Schedule and Results

Wisconsin	L	66-51	Iowa	W	95-81
Michigan	W	81-67*	Illinois	W	61-44*
Minnesota	W	71-55*	Minnesota	W	84-82
Illinois	W	51-49	Purdue	W	82-69*
Iowa	W	80-65*	Michigan	W	73-58
Indiana	W	73-59	Wisconsin	W	56-51*
Ohio State	W	76-71*	Purdue	W	60-46
Northwestern	W	65-48*			
Penn State	W	70-68	*MSU home game		

Road to the Final Four

Big Ten Season

CLEAVES, REBOUNDS SAVE MSU

MSU 70, PENN STATE 68

FEBRUARY 3, 1999
JACK EBLING

UNIVERSITY PARK—For three days, Tom Izzo was worried. He tried to tell his Michigan State players to prepare for Penn State's best basketball effort.

And he tried to warn anyone who'd listen about the danger of facing wounded Nittany Lions.

Today, Izzo has teeth marks as proof.

His team has something much more important, an eighth straight Big Ten triumph and a one-game lead over Wisconsin in the nation's best conference.

A 70-68 escape over a 10th-place team wasn't what anyone envisioned Tuesday.

But come February 28, the Spartans' third league road win might be a vision of beauty in the final standings.

For that, Izzo can thank a superior group of offensive rebounders and a point guard who showed up just in time.

After Penn State's volleyball team, an NCAA runner-up, was recognized at halftime, MSU kept the ball alive and had 12 of its 21 extra chances in the last 20 minutes.

The last of those tough rebounds and a quick assist by Andre Hutson allowed Mateen Cleaves to hit a tying 3-pointer with his team down 68-65.

Then, after Hutson played terrific defense and rebounded a miss by center Calvin Booth, Cleaves made amends for a subpar showing and made another All-America play.

His off-balance flip from 12 feet found nothing but net with .4-seconds left and let the Spartans prevail without their best showing.

"I feel very fortunate and lucky, to be honest," Izzo said. "I take my hat off to (Penn State coach) Jerry Dunn. I don't know if I could've gotten my team back up after what happened here Sunday."

The Lions lost 98-95 in double-overtime to Indiana on another prayer by a big-time player, guard A.J. Guyton.

So when everyone figured Penn State might be thinking about the start of spring football, Izzo had to wonder.

He heard Northwestern coach Kevin O'Neill call the Lions one of the league's best teams, despite four Big Ten losses by three points or less.

And he didn't want MSU to have to deliver heartbreak No. 5.

Izzo wanted to break the hosts' spirit early in a cavernous building that was more than half-empty.

Instead, Penn State fought back from 7-0 and 22-8 deficits, finally drew even in the second half and had a three-point lead and possession of the

All season long, Mateen Cleaves' clutch play has gotten the Spartans through some tense moments. At Penn State, Cleaves' shot with less than one second left provided the winning margin.

ball with 1:15 to play.

That's when the Spartans reminded us they're pretty tough heavyweight fighters, too.

And when Cleaves proved great players aren't always great—just big when they have to be.

"It's all Cleaves," radio analyst and ex-MSU coach Gus Ganakas had said at halftime, when Cleaves had two of his 14 points. "It's all up to him."

If Ganakas was a prophet, Izzo was a coach who recognized his team's greatest strength—rebounding and defense—and used it to leave with another W.

As in "Whew!"

"We're a very good offensive rebounding team," Izzo said. "That's one thing I will brag about. That's partly because we miss so many shots. We took the attitude that if we're going to miss that many, we better go get them."

MSU went and got the ball and grabbed a win that had almost slipped behind Mount Nittany.

It was a better performance against a better team than the Spartans had at Illinois, but the same result—a two-point victory that means as much this morning as a rout of Iowa or Indiana.

"It wasn't a lack of effort on our part," Dunn said of another crusher. "You've got to give the other guys some credit. . . . They've got some guys who were able to get it done."

Done, undone, then done the hard way.

Road to the Final Four

Big Ten Season

MSU "SCARY" IN 9TH WIN IN A ROW

MSU 95, IOWA 81

FEBRUARY 7, 1999
LARRY LAGE

IOWA CITY—When Mateen Cleaves made shot after shot from 3-point range this week in practice, Michigan State coach Tom Izzo joked that Cleaves wouldn't have anything left for Iowa.

He did.

Cleaves went 4-for-7 on 3-point shots and the Spartans played some of their best basketball of the season Saturday in a 95-81 pounding of the Hawkeyes before a quieted crowd of 15,500 at Carver-Hawkeye Arena.

"I guess he saved a few 3-pointers," Izzo said. "It was great to see him get off to a great start. I think that was one of the best games I've seen him play."

Cleaves finished with 14 points, nine assists, two steals and one turnover.

Morris Peterson led MSU with a career-high 27 points, on 9-for-12 shooting, off the bench.

As a team, the Spartans shot 57.9 percent (33-of-57) from the field and committed only 11 turnovers in a performance that impressed the home team.

"When Mateen Cleaves is on fire like that from the outside and everybody is clicking, they're a scary team," said Iowa's Guy Rucker, an Inkster native. "They're the best transition team in the country and when they're making 3-pointers, they're tough to stop."

"They're the best team I've played against in three years here."

The Spartans won their ninth straight and 16th out of their last 17 games. MSU is ranked No. 8 in both the USA TODAY/ESPN and Associated Press polls, but could move up after five teams ahead of the Spartans lost at least one game this week.

In the Spartans' two victories over Iowa this year, rough play was the norm. Here, Iowa's Jess Settles tries to wrestle the ball from State's Antonio Smith.

Road to the Final Four

Big Ten Season

BLOWOUT NEVER IN DOUBT

MSU 61, ILLINOIS 44

FEBRUARY 12, 1999
JACK EBLING

EAST LANSING—The signs of victory were everywhere. On and off the basketball court. There was only one question in the first half Thursday.

Who was having more fun, Tom Izzo's torrid team or Michigan State's festive fans?

A 61-44 smothering of Illinois was over before the first timeout.

It might have been over before the opening tip.

The Spartans were so much quicker than the Fighting Illini, the only real concern was boredom.

There could have been a much bigger margin if MSU had hit more than one basket in a span of 10:29.

Or if anyone had scored more than Thomas Kelley's 10 points—one for each conference win in a school-record-tying streak.

To be fair, it was tough to pick Illinois' biggest mistake of the evening.

But Lon Kruger's players had four major problems before reaching Breslin Center:

MSU's Thomas Kelley hits a two-point shot over Illinois defenders Arias Davis, left, and Cory Bradford.

They were correctly identified as last season's other Big Ten co-champion.

They scared MSU to the final tick—and even a few seconds after—in a 51-49 struggle on January 16.

They got the Spartans' full attention again with a win over Wisconsin Saturday.

And they decided to board a bus Wednesday for the Champaign, Illinois, airport.

Tom Izzo's team was so dominant on defense that the Illini had back-to-back shot-clock violations. When Illinois did manage to get shots away, it hit just 24 percent in the first half.

But this was an evening that MSU owned, regardless of the opposition.

Road to the Final Four

Big Ten Season

IT WAS A WIN FOR THE AGES

MSU 84, MINNESOTA 82

FEBRUARY 14, 1999
JACK EBLING

MINNEAPOLIS—They'll talk about this one forever. When Michigan state's 1998-99 basketball team has a 20-year reunion, they'll tell the story.

And when the Spartans hold their second centennial celebration, they'll have another cherished video.

If MSU didn't quite win the Big Ten title Saturday night at Minnesota, it won something else.

Everyone's respect.

An 84-82 triumph over the gutsy Golden Gophers was the type of win that builds reputations.

For another team, you could say it would build character.

Tom Izzo's guys already have that.

Trailing by 10 points in Williams Arena, with everything going against them, the Spartans dug deep and came up with answers.

Best of all, they left with a win.

In a game that would have to crack the top 16 in MSU basketball history, this one had it all.

Izzo's players could never stop Minnesota star Quincy Lewis—until they had to.

> **In a game that would have to crack the top 16 in MSU basketball history, this one had it all.**

They could never put the desperate Gophers back in their hole, the bowels of Williams Arena.

They couldn't silence a raucous crowd until the final .1 second ticked off.

Instead of leaving ticked off themselves at a wasted effort, the Spartans arrived home early this morning with the same two-game lead over Ohio State they had when the evening began.

A team that wasn't supposed to be able to win from the perimeter sizzled from 3-point range.

First, A.J. Granger.

Then, Mateen Cleaves.

Finally, Charlie Bell.

A blizzard of 3s fell on an otherwise balmy day in the Twin Cities.

But at winning time, with MSU up 80-79, the winners delivered the storm of the century at both ends, Antonio Smith stripping Lewis and alertly calling a time out.

On the in-bounds play, Bell broke loose for a slam

to make it a three-point game.

That's when Minnesota responded and turned a great game into a classic.

Terrance Simmons hit a 3 to tie it at 82, and leave everyone thinking overtime.

Everyone but Cleaves, that is.

Just as he did at Penn State, the reigning Big Ten Player of the Year showed why he ranks with the nation's best.

He took the ball through five Gophers because that was all they had on the court.

If Minnesota had played eight guys, Cleaves would have found a way to the basket.

Today, he's found something else, after a 23-point effort. Cleaves, Morris Peterson, Bell, Granger and everyone else in green and white have found a way to prove they belong.

They belong atop the conference standings.

They belong in the No. 4 spot in the polls.

And they belong on the tips of our tongues when we talk about the greatest teams in MSU history.

Yes, there's plenty of work to be done.

It'll take wins over Purdue Tuesday and at Michigan Thursday to allow the ideal scenario to occur. The Spartans could wrap up an outright conference title with a third victory next week, a win over Wisconsin in Breslin Center.

With every living basketball letterman and coach invited back, what better place to celebrate?

Michigan State's twin victories over Minnesota in 1999 featured some of the Spartans' most inspired play. At the Breslin Center, MSU's Morris Peterson gets tripped up by Minnesota's Kyle Sander as he drives to the basket.

And what better place to stamp themselves as one of the best than here, where Smith and Jason Klein became the first MSU players to win three times, forfeits not included.

The Spartans were the best on the floor, and are the best in the league.

Or at least the best on a glorious Saturday night when they had to be.

Road to the Final Four

Big Ten Season

SPARTANS SOLVE PURDUE

MSU 82, PURDUE 69

FEBRUARY 17, 1999
LARRY LAGE

EAST LANSING—The Purdue Boilermakers kept Michigan State from claiming an undisputed Big Ten title last year. This season, things are different.

The Spartans beat Purdue 82-69 Tuesday night in the Breslin Center.

MSU had to share the conference crown with Illinois last year after losing to the Boilermakers at home in the regular-season finale. The Spartans hadn't beaten Purdue at home since 1992.

MSU's Charlie Bell said those factors motivated the Spartans.

"They spoiled our victory party last year," said Bell, who had 13 points. "We wanted to see the highlights of the crowd rushing the floor like they did against Purdue (in 1990), but it didn't happen."

MSU moved two-and-a-half games ahead of Ohio State in the conference standings. If the Buckeyes lose tonight at Indiana, the Spartans will earn at least a share of the Big Ten title.

The Spartans, who are 13-0 at home, improved their school-record conference win streak to 12 games and have won 19 of their last 20 games. They are ranked No. 4 in both the USA TODAY/ESPN and Associated Press polls.

Jason Klein led MSU with 22 points. He scored 11 points in the first 3:02 of the second half and had seven points in a 57-second stint, which put the Boilermakers away.

Hutson added 11 points and six rebounds.

Mateen Cleaves led MSU's attack with eight points, on 4-of-6 shooting, and 11 assists.

The Spartans made 55.6 percent of their shots.

"Thank God for our shooting," MSU coach Tom Izzo said. "We're starting to play better because we're shooting better and when Mateen is running this team like he is, we're a better team."

MSU went on an 11-2 run to open the second half, which turned the Spartans' 12-point lead into a 50-29 edge with 16:58 remaining. It was an impressive stretch against the Boilermakers, ranked 18th/22nd.

The Spartans held Purdue without a field goal from the final 1:13 of the first half until the 14:22 mark of the second. They had little trouble maintaining command the rest of the game.

"Our guys played hard," Izzo said. "I was pleased with our performance."

After Purdue made its first attempt of the game, it missed the next seven shots. A 9-0 MSU run put the Spartans ahead 9-2 with 15:16 left in the first half. The Boilermakers sliced their deficit to 11-8 and tied the game at 13 with 11:21 remaining.

MSU outscored Purdue 11-2 over the next four minutes to take a 24-15 lead. The Spartans led 39-27 at halftime.

MSU led by as many as 23 points in the second half. Purdue starters outscored MSU's reserves 9-4 in the final minute to make the game appear closer than it was.

After Purdue spoiled MSU's title celebration last year, Andre Hutson, Charlie Bell and Mateen Cleaves (l to r) enjoy the drubbing that the Spartans handed out to the Boilermakers this season at the Breslin Center.

Football Anyone?

When told that Izzo has often said, "Just let my guys play as hard as Purdue," Keady seemed genuinely flattered.

But his team was flattened by MSU, which built a 23-point lead and coasted home for its 12th straight win.

"They were aggressive on defense," Keady said. "I really love that. The game was won in the first half with the way they got after loose balls on the floor."

For a football fanatic like Izzo, there was no greater compliment possible.

And from a former college football standout and NFL defensive back like Keady, it was a tribute straight from the heart.

"I wish we had a mandatory rule that kids had to go out for football," he said. "Except that all the mothers would hate me."

—Jack Ebling, February 17, 1999

Road to the Final Four

Big Ten Season

WIN GIVES SPARTANS SHARE OF BIG TEN TITLE

MSU 73, MICHIGAN 58

FEBRUARY 19, 1999
TOM GANTERT

EAST LANSING—They were screaming as loud as they could at the jumbo TV screen in the Breslin Center like some crazy uncle.

"Get in!" Michigan State senior Aaron Coombs yelled as he pounded his feet up and down while sitting on the bleachers.

"Get in!" Haslett's Steve Culp shouted as he jumped up and down.

MSU forward Jason Klein had just hit a 3-point basket. Michigan State was en route to beating rival Michigan 73-58 Thursday night, clinching a share of the Big Ten title.

Coombs was reminded that neither the players nor MSU coach Tom Izzo could hear his cheers. They were 60 miles away.

"Maybe Izzo can catch the vibes," Coombs said as he shook his head.

That was the message sent by 2,607 supporters who showed up to watch the conference championship clincher at Breslin.

They wanted to send good vibes and show support for their Spartans.

Most would have been at the game if they could have gotten tickets.

Instead, they chose to sit with their fellow fans, like children with their faces pressed against the window of a locked candy store.

"No tickets to the game," Karen Church of Lansing said.

But the Breslin Center was turned into East Lansing's largest living room with all eyes glued to four 8-foot by 12-foot screens.

Coombs, like most everyone else, would have preferred to be in Ann Arbor.

"I was supposed to be at the game," Coombs said. "This is the next best thing. That's half the point. To watch the game with the crowd."

Lansing's Brian Shiels, a MSU junior, could have watched the game from his apartment.

"But I'm here with 500 of my closest Spartan friends," Shiels said, his conversation occasionally drowned out by chants of "Go Green, Go White."

East Lansing's Kevin Hatch, an MSU senior, said

> "But I'm here with 500 of my closest Spartan friends," Shiels said, his conversation occasionally drowned out by chants of "Go Green, Go White."

this was more than just watching a game.

"It is letting the nation know what kind of school we are," Hatch said.

On Thursday, it was mostly loud.

With each Spartan basket, the crowd erupted, drowning out the ESPN telecast momentarily.

Objectivity was not on the agenda.

"They're a bunch of dirty punks and the only way they can win is to cheat," Hatch yelled to a friend after a Michigan foul.

LaTorsha Hill, an MSU freshman from Warren, was the first in line to get in the Breslin Center. She arrived at 5 p.m., two and a half hours before tipoff.

"I like to be first at everything," Hill said.

She came expecting no less from the Spartans.

She wasn't disappointed.

Late in the second half with their team ahead by 11 points, MSU fans started to sing to the opposing Wolverines.

"Nah-nah-nah-nah, nah-nah-nah-nah, hey-hey-hey, goodbye!

"Nah-nah-nah-nah, nah-nah-nah-nah, hey-hey-hey, goodbye!"

But Hatch wasn't quite ready to go. He had personal business to finish.

Years ago, Hatch came to the Breslin Center and watched Michigan's Chris Webber and Juwan Howard walk over the Spartan "S" emblem on midcourt and wipe their feet on it after beating the Spartans.

"You don't forget something like that," Hatch said.

And it was time for payback.

MSU basketball fans flood the floor at the Breslin Center after MSU defeated Michigan at Crisler Arena in Ann Arbor to claim at least a share of the Big Ten title.

"Hey," Haslett's Matt McDonald, an MSU junior and friend of Hatch, yelled over the singing students. "We have got to kiss the 'S.'"

Not just for themselves. But for the MSU players who would have wanted to do it but were 60 miles away.

"Yeah," Hatch said confidently. "We know security."

As the screen above showed an MSU player holding the ball as time expired, Hatch, McDonald and Shiels jumped onto the floor and made it to midcourt.

"Ahhhh!" they yelled as they jumped up and down on the S. "We're No. 1!"

Soon, 10 fans followed. Then 10 more. Then 20 more.

Hatch was soon swallowed by a sea of students wearing green and white and jumping up and down.

They didn't know most of them but there were no strangers on this night.

Just all their closest Spartan friends.

Road to the Final Four

Big Ten Season

WIN AS SWEET AS CAN BE

FEBRUARY 19, 1999
JACK EBLING

ANN ARBOR—It started at 7:16 p.m. in a green-draped Crisler Arena. And it stopped some time this morning on the basketball-crazy streets of East Lansing.

"Let's go State! ... Let's go State!" was the first chant from Sections 54 and 57.

Today, and forever more, there's another cheer, "Back-to-back ... Big Ten champs!"

The Michigan State Spartans took another step on a sturdy ladder of achievement Thursday.

And they did it in a perfect neutral setting, the home of their No. 1 rival.

A 73-58 victory over Michigan wasn't MSU's best performance.

But a 13th straight win gave the Spartans their eighth league title—and only their second back-to-back crowns—in 49 seasons of conference play.

It also brought just the sixth sweep of the Wolverines in 31 years.

> The Spartans' two wins over the Michigan Wolverines in 1999 gave MSU six straight victories over their No. 1 rival.

And deep inside, it eased the pain of so many setbacks. On the court, Michigan had often been dominant, even through the middle part of this decade.

But a third straight series win was the Spartans' ninth in 20 chances in the 1990s.

That's only impressive if you remember the Wolverines' 11-6 advantage prior to Feb. 17, 1998—and if you recall the gripes, "Izzo can't beat Michigan."

His teams had been thumped by 22, 29, 13, 20 and 10 points in his first five series opportunities.

After a Gatorade douse, as he talked of special efforts by special players, that pain was behind him.

He was finished crying about Chris Webber's recruitment.

And he was over the Wolverines' classless antics in Breslin during the "Fab Five" era.

It's a new day for Izzo and a great one for three seniors — Antonio Smith, Jason Klein and Thomas Kelley—who'd never experienced a win in Crisler.

For underclassmen Mateen Cleaves, Charlie Bell, Andre Hutson, Morris Peterson, A.J. Granger and Doug Davis.

And for "The Izzone" and everyone else in green, in Washtenaw, Ingham and every other county.

"This is very sweet," Smith said. "(Winning in Crisler) is something we've wanted to do for a long time. It's even sweeter to get a piece of the title here."

It wasn't as easy as the final score seemed.

MSU's Morris Peterson lands after slicing through the Michigan defense for two more points in the Spartans' season sweep of the Wolverines.

> **R**oad to the
> **F**inal **F**our
>
> Big Ten
> Season

TOTAL TITLE

MSU 56, WISCONSIN 51

FEBRUARY 22, 1999
LARRY LAGE

EAST LANSING—Before the season, Michigan State coach Tom Izzo said if the Spartans hoped to be successful, they couldn't lose their blue-collar attitude.

They didn't.

MSU scrapped its way to an outright Big Ten championship Sunday, fending off Wisconsin 56-51 Sunday in front of 14,659 delirious fans at the Breslin Center. The win gave the Spartans their second consecutive league title. Last year, they shared the crown with Illinois.

"This feels good," MSU forward Antonio Smith said. "We weren't satisfied last year, you know. We had to go out there and accept a trophy after just being beaten (by Purdue in the regular season finale)."

MSU set a modern (post-World War II) school record with its 14th consecutive win. It also tied a Big Ten record in the 1990s (with the 1993 Indiana Hoosiers) for consecutive conference wins in a season.

Their accomplishments prompted a wild celebration on the Breslin floor. Players hugged as students rushed the court. A metal ladder was set up under the south basket. Each Spartan, starting with the seniors, took a turn cutting down the net.

"I've never been on a championship team in my life," said MSU swingman Morris Peterson, who led the Spartans with 13 points. "That emotion was unbelievable. It was just overwhelming to me. And I'm so happy for coach. This was all his plan."

MSU, ranked No. 3 in the latest USA TODAY/ESPN poll and fourth by The Associated Press, has lost just once in the last 22 games.

It has shown it can win playing any style.

The Spartans prefer to run the fast break, but when teams take that away, as Wisconsin did, they adapt.

"Wisconsin forced us to play its slow-down, nitty-gritty style, but we beat them anyway," MSU guard Charlie Bell said. "They took a lot of things away from us, but they couldn't take our Big Ten title."

Both teams struggled early, missing seven of their first eight shots while scoring a combined six points in the first six minutes.

Wisconsin took an 8-6 lead at the 12:20 mark and led 17-12 seven minutes later. The Spartans didn't capture the advantage until Cleaves made two free throws with 2.2 seconds left in the half, giving MSU a 21-19 edge at the break.

Spartan guards Cleaves and Bell were 0-for-7 in the first half, while the Badgers' backcourt of Mason and Ty Calderwood was 0-for-6 from the field.

MSU took command with a 10-0 run to open the second half, giving it a 31-19 lead. Its defense held Wisconsin without a point until 15:25 remained.

Despite not making a field goal from the 13:53 mark until there was 8:53 left, MSU kept its lead between 14 and nine points.

Wisconsin cut its deficit to six points with 58.3 seconds left, but MSU made 5-of-8 free throws in the waning moments to seal the victory.

"Emotionally, we laid it on the line," Wisconsin coach Dick Bennett said. "There were a couple of key moments before halftime where we got a good look. But their stretch to open the second half is a credit to them. They got their running game going and played like a champ."

MSU's Mateen Cleaves leaps off the ground as time runs out in MSU's win over Wisconsin for sole possession of the Big Ten regular season basketball championship.

Road to the Final Four

Big Ten Season

WEEKEND A WINNER FOR ALL

FEBRUARY 22, 1999
JACK EBLING

EAST LANSING—They've changed the shape of Breslin Center. From an oval to a giant heart. But the Michigan State Spartans gave as much love as they got Sunday.

They capped a surreal centennial celebration with an outright Big Ten basketball title.

They won in throwback jerseys, with a throwback style that made sweat more important than sweetness.

And they showed seven decades of predecessors just how far a program has come—and how far it might be going.

A 56-51 win over stubborn Wisconsin was a triumph of will more than skill.

It was a perfect example of Izzoball on an ideal MSU weekend.

The Badgers had to think the Spartans were more physical on defense than UCLA was in the Rose Bowl.

And as the winners let their leader snip the final strand of net and wave it to the crowd, you could hear him holler "Thank you!"

To his players, to their fans and to the world.

Seconds later, Big Ten Commissioner Jim Delany made a different sort of trophy presentation—a joyous gift compared to last year's dud.

"It's great to be here today to congratulate and honor the OUTRIGHT 1999 Big Ten Champs," he said. "To celebrate the last year of the century with an outright championship, what a great gift to give your university."

To Izzo's university now and to a school that will send Antonio Smith, Jason Klein and Thomas Kelley off to the real world as unquestioned successes.

To the launching pad for 503 basketball lettermen and 15 other head coaches—with most of the living in

> MSU basketball players Thomas Kelley, left, and Steve Cherry, right, hold up the Spartans' Big Ten Championship trophy and celebrate with thousands of fans at the Breslin Center.

attendance and the others looking on.

And to a future that's every bit as bright as the past and a precious present.

"I just want to say a couple of things," Izzo said, saluting his parents, his mentor, Jud Heathcote, and his players. "The administration here has been unbelievable. But this community, 'The Izzone' and you fans are second to none!"

The beauty is he wasn't pandering.

Ex-Spartan player and assistant Edgar Wilson, the head coach at Ferris State, said as much as the party continued on the floor.

"This team has tremendous heart and resiliency," Wilson said. "But this environment is really something. With the support they have, it's a tremendous advantage. And what Tom has really done is bring everything together and bring everyone back."

Today, the Spartans and Boilermakers stand one win behind Indiana—and 10 ahead of Michigan—for the best Big Ten regular-season record in the 1990s.

If he didn't have enough reason to smile, that fact ought to make Heathcote happy.

As his protege ruled the Big Ten kingdom, Heathcote looked as thrilled as anyone had seen him since a win over Notre Dame 20 years ago meant a trip to the Final Four.

Maybe he realized it's about time for another one.

Road to the Final Four

Big Ten Season

MSU fans in the Izzone student cheering section cheer on the Spartan basketball team in the first half against Wisconsin.

MSU's Doug Davis drives the lane with three Wisconsin defenders all over him. Left to right are Wisconsin's Charlie Wills (40), Mike Kelley (22) and Hennssy Auriatal (5).

Fans get a chance to touch the Big Ten trophy held by MSU's Antonio Smith (above) and to celebrate with their Spartan heroes (right) after MSU defeated Wisconsin for sole possession of the Big Ten Championship.

Road to the Final Four

Big Ten Season

SPARTANS ROLLING, POUND PURDUE

MSU 60, PURDUE 46

MARCH 1, 1999
LARRY LAGE

WEST LAFAYETTE—Big Ten regular season champion Michigan State crept closer to securing a No. 1 seed for the NCAA Tournament on Sunday by downing Purdue 60-46 at Mackey Arena.

The Spartans won their school-record 15th consecutive game and their 22nd in 23 contests. MSU moved to No. 2 in the USA TODAY/ESPN poll, its highest ranking since winning the national championship in 1979.

"I think we made a statement about what we want and what we think we deserve," MSU forward Morris Peterson said. "We've built a lot of momentum for the tournaments and I can't think of a better time to be peaking like we are."

The Spartans are the top seed in this week's Big Ten Tournament at the United Center in Chicago. MSU's first game will be against the winner of the Northwestern-Penn State game at 3 p.m. Friday.

MSU coach Tom Izzo said he doesn't believe his team has a No. 1 NCAA seed locked up.

> "I think we made a statement about what we want and what we think we deserve," MSU forward Morris Peterson said. "We've built a lot of momentum for the tournaments and I can't think of a better time to be peaking like we are."

"I think we deserve to be one, but who knows," he said. "We have to wait until after the Big Ten Tournament because you're judged on your last game.

"But I think this really helped us."

The Spartans have used varied styles and different heroes en route to the conference crown.

Senior power forward Antonio Smith led the way against Purdue, scoring 12 points and pulling down eight rebounds.

Point guard Mateen Cleaves and Peterson added eight points each. Guards Charlie Bell and Doug Davis scored seven apiece. Forwards Andre Hutson and A.J. Granger chipped in six points each.

"I thought our guys showed a lot of grit and determination to win this game any way possible," Izzo said. "We have no real egos on this team and we have been able to accomplish a lot because of that."

MSU seized the momentum when Davis scored the final five points of the first half, giving the Spartans a 24-21 lead.

After the Boilers tied the game at 30 with 15:24 left, the Spartans blew the game open by outscoring them 26-9 over the next 10 minutes. MSU's reserves scored 10 points during the stretch and outscored Purdue's bench 23-2.

The Spartans outrebounded the Boilers 39-20, 14-6 on the offensive glass.

"Rebounding was the biggest killer for us," Purdue coach Gene Keady said.

"I feel fortunate to win this game," Izzo said. "Both teams came out kind of sluggish and I thought we looked a little out of sync. I think both defenses shut down both offenses."

MSU played its first game in a week after battling five teams in the previous 11 days.

Every game with the Boilermakers brings a fiery and respectful coaching matchup between Purdue's Gene Keady and MSU's Tom Izzo. The tough-nosed battles between these two teams have been described as "football on wood."

Road to the Final Four

Big Ten Tournament

MSU 61, NORTHWESTERN 59

SPARTANS CAN'T STOP ESCHMEYER

MARCH 6, 1999
GERRY AHERN

CHICAGO—Michigan State didn't allow Evan Eschmeyer to beat them Friday in the quarterfinals of the Big Ten Tournament.

But boy, did he come close to doing so.

The sixth-year senior center scored 30 points in the Wildcats' 61-59 loss to the top-seeded Spartans. If not for an Eschmeyer disappearing act in the final 3:06, MSU might have made a first-round exit from the conference tourney for the second consecutive year.

"They went in to Eschmeyer every time, just like they have for the past three years," MSU coach Tom Izzo said. "We didn't guard him at all. It's not that we didn't try. He was just better than us."

At least until the final 186 seconds.

Eschmeyer made 11-of-16 field goal attempts and 8-of-8 free throws, almost singlehandedly willing a Wildcat upset.

A combination of a more concentrated defensive effort by the Spartans and some bad decisions by the freshmen in the Northwestern backcourt kept the ball out of Eschmeyer's hands at crunch time.

"We got away from going to Esch down the stretch," Northwestern coach Kevin O'Neill said. "Part of that is us being young. Part of that is Michigan State."

Eschmeyer, who struck for 20 points in the second half, said he would have liked to have seen the ball more with the game on the line.

Fortunately for MSU, he didn't.

"Eschmeyer is the best guy I've ever faced in the post," MSU forward Andre Hutson said. "He gets the ball and you get the feeling that you're really going to have to come up with something big every time to stop him."

Hutson and MSU came up with just enough on Friday.

> "We didn't guard him at all. It's not that we didn't try. He was just better than us."

Road to the Final Four

Big Ten Tournament

CLOSING IN ON A CROWN

MSU 56, WISCONSIN 41

MARCH 7, 1999
LARRY LAGE

CHICAGO— Michigan State decided it was through allowing Wisconsin to dictate Saturday's Big Ten Tournament semifinal.

After a half of playing at the Badgers' preferred snail-like pace, the Spartans' defense took over in the second half en route to a convincing 56-41 victory at the United Center.

The Spartans, ranked No. 2 in both the USA TODAY/ESPN and Associated Press polls, have won 17 straight games and appear to be a lock for a No. 1 seed when the NCAA Tournament pairings are announced.

After struggling through the first 20 minutes, the Spartans took command with a 12-0 run to start the second half to take a 34-22 lead. The game was never in doubt from there.

"We got our running game going off of our defense," MSU coach Tom Izzo said. "Maybe they got tired when we kept running fresh bodies in." Wisconsin shot a season-worst 29.3 percent from the field, just one day after shooting a season-best 61.5 percent in a win over Iowa. The Badgers were held without a point from the 3:30 mark of the first half to the 13:16 mark of the second.

After the Spartans' opening second-half run, they maintained an advantage that hovered between 10 and 18 points the rest of the game.

"I think the second half was a good wake-up call for us," A.J. Granger said.

> Once the Spartans got their running game going against the Badgers, it was on to the finals for MSU.

Road to the Final Four

Big Ten Tournament

MSU 67, ILLINOIS 50

SPARTANS ROUT ILLINI FOR BIG TEN TITLE

MARCH 8, 1999
LARRY LAGE

CHICAGO—Four down—one to go. The Michigan State basketball team achieved the fourth of five season goals Sunday, winning the Big Ten Tournament championship, 67-50, over Illinois at the United Center.

The Spartans (29-4) entered the tournament with three goals accomplished: the Big Ten regular-season title and championships in the Coca-Cola and Pearl Harbor classics.

"It's one thing to tell the world about your goals, it's another thing to accomplish them," MSU coach Tom Izzo said. "They really wanted to win the Big Ten regular-season title and tournament title and they went out and worked hard to do it. That's the most satisfying thing.

"I think (Big Ten commissioner) Jim Delany said it best when he said, 'This is not a flash-in-the-pan team. They did it in December, January, February and March.'"

MSU extended its school-record winning streak to 18 games. It also surpassed the 1989-90 Spartans for most wins in a season.

Those two feats are bonuses to the four goals already accomplished.

The final goal will be the toughest to achieve—winning the national championship.

"We would've been disappointed if we didn't reach all of our goals so far," MSU forward Antonio Smith said. "But we really can focus our attention to trying to win the national championship now."

MSU enters the NCAA Tournament as the No. 1 seed in the Midwest Region. The Spartans begin their title quest on Friday against Mount St. Mary's in Milwaukee.

Spartans point guard Mateen Cleaves was named the Big Ten Tournament's Most Outstanding Player. Cleaves had nine points and 10 assists against Illinois. He finished the three-game weekend with 29 points, 29 assists and just five turnovers.

"My stats look good, but my teammates made my job easy," Cleaves said. "They ran the floor well and knocked down shot after shot."

Smith joined Cleaves on the all-tournament team. He grabbed 13 rebounds and had nine points against the Illini. For the tourney, he had 32 rebounds and 23 points.

Cory Bradford (Illinois), Michael Redd (Ohio

> "It's one thing to tell the world about your goals, it's another thing to accomplish them," MSU coach Tom Izzo said.

State) and Evan Eschmeyer (Northwestern) rounded out the all-tournament team.

The Illini never led, but tied the game twice and cut their deficit to one point four times in the first nine minutes.

The Spartans held the rebounding edge early and maintained it throughout the game. They outrebounded Illinois 9-2 in the first six minutes, with six offensive rebounds, and finished with a 40-24 advantage. MSU scored 20 points off 18 offensive rebounds.

"We knew they were going to be tired after playing three games in the last three days so we really wanted to dominate on the boards," MSU forward Andre Hutson said. "As the game went on, we could tell they were tired because it became easy to get rebounds."

MSU put away the Illini with a 7-0 run from the 7:30 to the 4:04 mark of the first half, building a 28-19 lead.

The Spartans led 38-25 at halftime.

They turned the game into a blowout in the first five minutes of the second half.

MSU held Illinois scoreless for the first 4:47, making a 9-0 run. The Spartans built a 47-25 lead.

They led by as many as 26 points and didn't let the Illini get closer than 15 points the rest of the game.

Hutson had 11 points and six rebounds. Morris Peterson and Thomas Kelley scored 11 and nine points respectively off the bench.

Bradford led Illinois (14-18) with 26 points.

The Spartans shot 47.5 percent from the field while holding Illinois to 39.5 percent shooting.

MSU guard Charlie Bell said the team was pleased to achieve its latest goal.

"We had a sour taste in our mouths last year after sharing the regular-season title with Illinois and losing our first game here in the Big Ten Tournament to Minnesota," said Bell, who had six points and three steals. "This feels great."

Reaching the final goal would feel even better.

High-flying MSU forward Morris Peterson led the Spartans' scoring attack all season long. Against Illinois, Peterson flew past the Illini's Victor Chukwudebe.

Road to the Final Four

Big Ten Tournament

MSU's Mateen Cleaves eyes the basket during the championship game of the Big Ten Tournament against Illinois.

Spartan fans congratulate MSU players after their victory in the Big Ten Tournament in Chicago.

Let the celebrations begin, Charlie Bell (left) and Mateen Cleaves (right).

Road to the Final Four

Big Ten Tournament

Mateen Cleaves helps cut down the net as he celebrates the Spartans' victory in the Big 10 Tournament with a win over Illinois.

Big Ten Championship Tournament March 7, 1999
United Center, Chicago

Illinois	25	25	—	50
MSU	38	29	—	67

Illinois (50)	min.	fg m-a	ft m-a	rb o-t	a	pf	tp
Krupalia	27	0-1	0-0	2-2	2	0	0
McClain	30	2-5	2-5	1-1	2	0	6
Chukwudebe	20	1-1	1-2	0-1	0	1	3
Bradford	36	7-17	1-2	1-3	0	0	21
Johnson	27	3-7	3-5	0-2	1	4	9
Hawkins	20	3-6	3-6	2-6	1	3	9
Mast	4	0-0	0-0	0-0	0	0	0
Archibald	13	0-1	0-0	0-3	2	1	0
Brown	23	1-5	0-0	1-2	2	3	2
Totals	200	17-43	10-20	7-20	10	12	50

Percentages: FG-.395, FT-.500. 3-Point Goals: 6-14, .429 (Bradford 6-9, Krupalija 0-1, McClain 0-1, Brown 0-3). Turnovers: 16. Steals: 10.

Michigan State (62)	min.	fg m-a	ft m-a	rb o-t	a	pf	tp
Klein	21	2-9	0-0	0-1	3	2	6
Hutson	25	4-7	3-4	2-6	1	1	11
A Smith	33	4-6	1-2	5-13	2	3	9
Cleaves	31	4-6	0-0	0-0	10	2	9
Bell	23	3-6	0-0	1-1	1	0	6
Kelley	12	4-7	0-0	1-1	1	1	9
Guess	1	0-1	0-0	0-0	0	0	0
B. Smith	1	0-1	0-0	0-0	0	0	0
Cherry	1	0-1	0-0	0-0	0	0	0
Davis	9	0-2	0-0	0-0	1	2	0
Peterson	22	5-10	0-0	5-10	0	3	11
Granger	21	2-3	2-4	1-2	1	2	6
Totals	200	28-59	6-10	16-35	20	16	67

Percentages: FG-.475, FT-.600. 3-Point Goals: 5-18, 278 (Klein 2-7, Cleaves 1-3, Bell 0-2, Kelley 1-2, Cherry 0-1, Davis 0-1, Peterson 1-2). Turnovers: 15. Steals: 9.

Attendance: 19,581.

Road to the Final Four
1ST ROUND
NCAA

MSU ROLLS INTO ROUND 2

MSU 76, MOUNT ST. MARY'S 53

MARCH 13, 1999
LARRY LAGE

MILWAUKEE—"Let's pick it up! Let's pick it up!" Michigan State's Mateen Cleaves had seen enough when he shouted those orders to his teammates Friday night.

The message was heard loud and clear.

The No. 1-seeded Spartans recovered after a slow start and trounced 16th-seeded Mount St. Mary's 76-53 in the first round of the NCAA Tournament's Midwest Regional at the Bradley Center.

MSU was tied or trailed the Mountaineers (15-15) for more than five of the game's first seven minutes.

The Spartans continued to struggle and seemed out of sync until Cleaves screamed his words of encouragement after getting fouled and hitting a layup with 7:25 left in the half. The junior All-American completed the 3-point play to give MSU a 22-16 lead.

The Spartans were in command from then out.

"We were playing too laid back," Cleaves said. "I didn't think any of us were playing with the effort we need to in this tournament."

> "We were playing too laid back," Cleaves said. "I didn't think any of us were playing with the effort we need to in this tournament."

The play came in the midst of MSU's decisive 14-2 run, which put it ahead 25-16.

Junior A.J. Granger came off the bench to lead the Spartans with a game-high 15 points. Antonio Smith scored 14 points and grabbed a game-high 12 rebounds. Andre Hutson added 11 points and Jason Klein had nine.

Cleaves scored eight points and had eight assists and led the second-half defensive effort against Mount St. Mary's leading scorer Gregory Harris, who scored just one of his 12 points after halftime.

MSU outrebounded Mount St. Mary's 46-22 overall and 16-8 on the offensive end.

"They don't appear to be that big, but they're so quick and have an amazing ability to get to the ball," Mount St. Mary's Tony Hayden said. "That's what was really killing us."

MSU made 50 percent of its shots and held the Mountaineers to 32-percent shooting.

Morris Peterson, who had eight points off the bench, said the early lackluster effort must be a wake-up call for the Spartans.

"Our goal is to win the national championship, but we didn't come close to giving championship-type effort tonight," he said. "Coach (Tom Izzo) really let us have it during timeouts and at halftime."

Izzo said it will take 40 minutes of good basketball from all of his players to achieve their lofty goals.

"I know what it will take to get us there and the way we started won't do it," he said. "We weren't sharp and we didn't do the things we talked about doing early like getting and taking good shots."

Charlie Bell sprained his left ankle with 13:08 left in the game. He said he did not know how serious the injury was, but expected to play Sunday.

Mount St. Mary's led 2-0, 4-2 and 8-7 in the first five minutes. The Spartans missed eight of their first 11 shots, while the Mountaineers made five of their first nine attempts.

There were four ties until MSU took the lead for good, 17-14, on a Thomas Kelley 3-pointer at the 12:30 mark.

The Spartans went from down three to up nine (25-16) over a 7:28 stint. MSU held Mount St. Mary's without a point for a 4:35 stretch.

MSU outscored the Mountaineers 11-3 in the final 4:20 of the half to take a 38-24 lead at halftime.

The Spartans opened the second half with an 8-0 run to put the game out of reach.

MSU led by as much as 32 points and did not allow the Mountaineers closer than 19 in the final 17 minutes.

"When Mateen was screaming at us, it gave us a final wake-up call," Kelley said. "He said what was needed to be said. Now we need to learn from this and not let it happen again."

MSU's Morris Peterson hits a three-point shot over a Mt. St. Mary's defender in the NCAA Tournament.

Road to the Final Four
2nd ROUND
NCAA

NCAA Tournament

MSU 74, MISSISSIPPI 66

SPARTANS TURN BACK MISSISSIPPI

MARCH 15, 1999
LARRY LAGE

MILWAUKEE—Tom Izzo's body language told the story of an emotion-packed game.

Michigan State's coach went from exasperated to worried to ecstatic with varying degrees of intensity—and he didn't hide his emotions once.

The top-seeded Spartans gave Izzo a reason to exude pride after beating ninth-seeded Mississippi 74-66 Sunday afternoon in the second round of the NCAA Midwest Regional at the Bradley Center.

"He's so into the game it seems like he's out on the court playing with us," Antonio Smith said. "We play through his personality. We couldn't do what we did today or have all season without him."

The win advances the Spartans to the Sweet 16 of the NCAA Tournament for the second straight year for the first time since the Earvin "Magic" Johnson-led teams in 1978 and 1979 accomplished the feat. MSU's 20th-consecutive victory also gave it enough wins to tie five other Big Ten teams for the second most in conference history.

MSU didn't beat the Rebels (20-13) as easily as the final score might indicate.

There were 19 lead changes and nine ties in a game that was played at an up-tempo pace with bodies colliding more often than baskets were scored.

Mateen Cleaves sparked the Spartans' game-deciding 13-0 run after Mississippi took a 59-56 lead on a

> "People can say a lot of things about his game, but they better always say that he's a winner," Izzo said.

Jason Harrison 3-pointer with 4:53 left.

Cleaves made a 3-pointer, two layups, two assists and a steal in a span of 3:05 during the decisive burst.

"People can say a lot of things about his game, but they better always say that he's a winner," Izzo said. "He may be 2-for-12 one game or he may do this or that, but all the kid does is win games."

Cleaves led MSU with 18 points, seven assists and three steals. The junior point guard had six turnovers, but only three in the final 35 minutes.

The Spartans wanted to take advantage of their superior front line and the strategy worked.

Andre Hutson scored 13 points, while Antonio Smith and A.J. Granger had nine each. The power-forward trio were a combined 11-of-19 from the field and 8-of-10 from the line.

Morris Peterson had 11 points, eight rebounds and three assists. The junior forward started in place of Charlie Bell, who was limited to 14 minutes with a left ankle sprain.

MSU made 47.2 percent of its shots. It held Ole Miss to 42.9 percent accuracy overall and 27.3 on 3-point shots. The Spartans outrebounded the Rebels 36-29 after getting beat on the boards in the first several minutes.

After the Spartans led 8-6 three minutes into the game, they did not lead again until they went ahead 27-26 with 3:02 left in the first half.

The Rebels led 32-29 at halftime.

There were five lead changes in the first three minutes of the second half. MSU led from the 17:00 mark until the Rebels tied the game at 54 with 6:14 left. Cleaves' key 3-pointer tied the game for the last time at 59 with 4:54 left.

"I never thought about us losing the game," Cleaves said. "I just knew that we were going to leave everything we had on that floor and that it would turn out OK."

The athletic and feisty Rebels did not allow Izzo to relax or celebrate for one second during the first 38 minutes of the game.

But Izzo leaped a couple feet into the air with both arms and fists extended high over his head when Peterson made a 15-foot shot after a timeout with two minutes left to play to put MSU ahead by eight points.

"That was a great moment," Izzo said. "We set that play up in our timeout. Three-fourths of the time it doesn't work out the way you want it to, but that play was executed perfectly.

"That took a little pressure off the game, but the pressure is not off this team yet. We're going to keep the pressure on because we haven't achieved what we set out to do yet."

MSU coach Tom Izzo and Mateen Cleaves celebrate and wave to the crowd after the Spartan win over Ole Miss.

Road to the Final Four

2nd ROUND

NCAA

MSU 74, Mississippi 66

(right) MSU's Charlie Bell, left, and Thomas Kelley, right, celebrate as the Spartans beat Ole Miss

Road to the Final Four
3rd ROUND
NCAA

MSU 54, OKLAHOMA 46

SPARTANS JOIN ELITE

MARCH 20, 1999
LARRY LAGE

NCAA Tournament

ST. LOUIS—The Michigan State Spartans have accomplished something that hasn't happened to the basketball program since the 1979 national championship season.

They're in the Elite Eight of the NCAA Tournament.

But they're not satisfied with the feat.

The Spartans slugged their way past Oklahoma 54-46 Friday night in the Sweet 16 at the Trans World Dome.

"We'll only enjoy this for a few minutes because we feel like we're at least a Final Four team," Charlie Bell said. "We have a golden opportunity to get to the Final Four and that's a once-in-a-lifetime opportunity that we've dreamed about since we were kids.

"The Elite Eight is nice, but it's not where we want our season to finish."

> "The Elite Eight is nice, but it's not where we want our season to finish."

MSU coach Tom Izzo wishes his players would enjoy the accomplishments that they've already achieved a little more than they were Friday night.

The Spartans tied a Big Ten record for wins with the 32-0 Indiana team from 1975-76. And the back-to-back conference champions have won 21 straight games.

"It's good that they're focused on their ultimate goal, but they've done some unbelievable things this year," Izzo said. "They should be proud of what they've done."

The top-seeded Spartans won despite making 40 percent of their shots because they held the 13th-seeded Sooners to 33.3 percent shooting. After being outbounded early, MSU finished with a 36-31 advantage on the boards.

Andre Hutson led MSU with 12 points and five rebounds. He made all three of his field goals and was 6-of-10 from the line.

Morris Peterson and A.J. Granger scored 11 and 10 points respectively to outscore Oklahoma's bench 21-7.

Mateen Cleaves missed 11-of-14 shots and scored nine points. The junior point guard had six turnovers and two assists.

"The only statistic that matters with Mateen is our wins and losses," senior Jason Klein said. "He may not have a pretty game, but he finds a way for us to win."

The Spartans and the Sooners exchanged leads 13 times and were tied five times in the first half. MSU's biggest lead was two points, while the Sooners led by four with 3:11 left in the half.

The Spartans outscored Oklahoma 7-2 to close the half and take a 26-25 lead. Cleaves missed his first eight shots, but gave MSU the halftime lead with a layup with 1.6 seconds left.

Granger was a major reason MSU was able to earn the lead despite its sluggish start. The junior forward scored all 10 of his points, on 4-of-4 shooting, in the first half.

"I've been playing well lately because I've been determined to give us an offensive spark," Granger said. "I was hot and the guys did a good job of getting me the ball."

MSU took command of the game with a 6-0 run to start the second half and take a 32-25 lead. Oklahoma was held scoreless for the first 3:45 and made just two of its first 12 shots.

The Sooners cut their deficit to 32-29 with 15:34 left, but were unable to get any closer. The Spartans' lead hovered between four and 10 points the rest of the game.

MSU's Morris Peterson saves the ball from going out of bounds in front of Oklahoma's Eric Martin during MSU's 54-46 win in the NCAA Midwest Regional in St. Louis.

Road to the Final Four

3rd ROUND

NCAA

COLLISION LEAVES FANS BREATHLESS

MARCH 20, 1999
GERRY AHERN

ST. LOUIS—It was the kind of moment that leaves you with a sick feeling in the pit of your stomach.

Like watching two speeding cars crash.

Michigan State point guard Mateen Cleaves and Oklahoma power forward Eduardo Najera were lying face down on the Trans World Dome court Friday night.

A brutal collision at 9:34 of the second half left the standout players crumpled on the floor.

Cleaves, who plowed full-speed into a Najera pick, came to rest by the MSU foul line.

Najera was about 8 feet away, knocked out cold with blood gushing from his chin.

A 10-minute delay ensued as fans, players and coaches of both teams held their collective breaths.

Oklahoma team doctor Brock Schnebel, wearing a pair of latex gloves, stitched a gash the length of Najera's chin. Sooners trainer Alex Brown steadied Najera's head as the doctor plunged the needle through the player's skin six times. The 6-foot-8, 235-pounder out of Chihuahua, Mexico's legs quivered with each stitch.

The game, which MSU led 36-31, suddenly seemed unimportant.

"He was conscious when I got to him and responsive," Brown said. "All X-rays were negative and he will be further evaluated today."

Then came the good news. Cleaves, looking glassy-eyed like a punch-drunk fighter, was ushered back to the MSU bench.

A few minutes later, OU guard Michael Johnson and coach Kelvin Sampson flanked Najera, who wrapped his arms around them and

> "When you see him face down with blood pouring out of his chin, it makes you realize what these kids mean to you."
> Sampson said.

walked off the court.

"When you see him face down with blood pouring out of his chin, it makes you realize what these kids mean to you." Sampson said.

Later, there was better news. Cleaves, with a bruised forehead, checked back into the game with 6:54 left.

Najera, who suffered a concussion, a bruised left breast bone and a laceration of his chin, returned at the 4:25 mark.

For the time being, the focus was back on basketball.

The Spartans went on to win the game 54-46, earning a berth in the NCAA Elite Eight for the first time since 1979.

More importantly, they knew that both their star Cleaves, and the Sooners' Najera were going to be OK.

Cleaves, who finished with nine points and two assists, came out of the collision a lot better than Najera. A bump on his head, which he said he'd treat by sleeping on a bag of ice, was the lone battle scar.

"I was a little dazed, but I wasn't knocked out," he said. "I was surprised, really, but I was OK.

"They asked me to count down from 100 by seconds, but my math isn't too good," he laughed.

With both players all right, a little levity was welcome.

Teammates Morris Peterson and Charlie Bell tend to an injured Mateen Cleaves after his vicious collision with Oklahoma's Eduardo Najera. The bloody collision of these two stars caused a 10-minute delay in the second half of the game.

Road to the Final Four

3rd ROUND

NCAA

Coach Tom Izzo talks to Mateen Cleaves in the heat of the battle vs. Oklahoma in the third round of the NCAA tournament.

Charlie Bell pulls a rebound away from Oklahoma's Eduardo Najera.

Road to the Final Four

4th ROUND

NCAA

NCAA Tournament

IT WAS A WIN FOR THE AGES

MSU 73, KENTUCKY 66

MARCH 22, 1999
JACK EBLING

ST. LOUIS—It was the greatest win by the greatest team in a century of Spartan basketball.

And when they celebrate in 2099, they'll talk about the day Michigan State silenced the Commonwealth of Kentucky.

A 73-66 win over the Wildcats Sunday meant more than just a trip to the Final Four for Tom Izzo's program.

It was a validation for the nation's No. 2 team, a muzzle for all remaining doubters and a Big Ten-record 33rd triumph.

But the best part for anyone with a drop of green blood was the way MSU did it:

By beating the No. 1 team in NCAA Tournament history and a group of fourth-year seniors who were 20-1 with two national titles.

By overcoming a 17-4 deficit and outscoring Division I's deepest squad 69-49 in the last 32:35.

And by ruining the weekend for roughly 30,000 Kentucky fans.

A popular shirt in a sea of blue said, "We don't just play college basketball …" on the front and "We ARE college basketball!" on the back.

Next weekend, they'll be CBS viewers like everyone else without a ticket to Tropicana Field in St. Petersburg, Florida, for the Big Ten Invitational—Ohio State-Connecticut and an MSU-Duke rematch.

> "I took Antonio to Michigan State," Izzo said, enjoying a buffet of emotions. "Now, he's taking me to the Final Four. …"

The Midwest's No. 1 seed, a point-and-a-half underdog, earned its second shot at the Blue Devils with a comeback like its 45-21 second half against the Wildcats in a 1957 Mideast Region final in Lexington, Kentucky.

And if it didn't completely erase the pain of a 52-49 loss to the same megapower in a Mideast final 21 years ago, it came pretty close for the likes of Jud Heathcote, Earvin Johnson and Terry Donnelly.

"We owed Kentucky!" said Donnelly, the hero of the 1979 championship win over Indiana State. "But when I look at this year's team, the big thing I see is character. They all pull for one another."

Like redshirt forward David Thomas, who must have jumped 40 inches when Morris Peterson swished the third and fourth of six straight free throws in the last half-minute.

Like Peterson's dad, Morris Sr., who guaranteed an MSU win before the game and nearly nailed the score as "Put 'Mo Pete' in St. Pete" became an itinerary, not just a slogan.

Like Johnson, who could be heard screaming all the way across the court, before beaming with pride: "I knew A.J. Granger would be a key. But Peterson was a man! ... And if anyone still wonders, the streak is 22 in a row."

Like Heathcote, who waited with a wide smile for Izzo to finish an on-court interview, then could barely contain himself when he congratulated his protege.

Izzo wasn't able to do that when met with two other men who've helped make him: Carl Izzo, a father so proud he chewed out Billy Packer for Spartans everywhere, and Antonio Smith, the original "Flintstone."

When it was time for Izzo to snip the final strand of net, he refused until he was joined on the ladder by Smith, a warrior who isn't through battling.

"I took Antonio to Michigan State," Izzo said, enjoying a buffet of emotions. "Now, he's taking me to the Final Four. ... But to do this with my family, with Jud and with Magic here is a dream."

It was also sweet reality.

MSU's Mateen Cleaves steals the ball from Kentucky's Tayshaun Price in the Midwest Regional Final of the NCAA tournament.

Road to the Final Four
4th ROUND
NCAA

Magic Johnson, center, helps to lead the Spartan cheers against Kentucky.

MSU's Antonio Smith grabs a rebound away from Kentucky's Heshimu Evans.

MSU's Antonio Smith and head coach Tom Izzo celebrate in St. Louis after beating Kentucky.

MSU's Morris Peterson beats Kentucky's Scott Padgett to the basket for a score.

Road to the Final Four

4th ROUND

NCAA

UN-FOUR-GETTABLE

MARCH 22, 1999
LARRY LAGE

ST. LOUIS—Michigan State senior Antonio Smith was irate. The Spartans were down 13 points in the first half to Kentucky when Smith, sensing a sour end to his college basketball career, ripped into his teammates during a timeout.

What did the muscle-bound forward say?

"Nothing you can print," he said with a sly grin. "I wanted to start grabbing people, but I just grabbed a towel and started hollering. Basically, I just told them we had been through too much and come too far not to play more aggressively."

The ploy worked.

Top-seeded Michigan State beat third-seeded Kentucky 73-66 Sunday night in the NCAA Midwest Regional finals before a record crowd of 42,519 in the Trans World Dome.

The Spartans advanced to the Final Four for the first time since Earvin "Magic" Johnson led the program to the national championship in 1979.

MSU coach Tom Izzo thoroughly enjoyed Smith's outburst.

"It was great," he said. "I just sat down in my chair, put my clipboard up, folded my arms and listened."

Smith's teammates responded by outscoring the Wildcats 67-49 over the final 31:49.

The Spartans didn't give up the lead after sophomore Andre Hutson converted a 70-foot pass from Cleaves for a layup with 7:30 left. That gave the Spartans a 55-54 lead.

Junior Morris Peterson was named Most Outstanding Player of the Midwest Region. He led the Spartans with 19 points and 10 rebounds.

He was joined on the All-Tournament team by teammates Cleaves and A.J. Granger, along with Kentucky's Scott Padgett and Wally Szczerbiak of Miami (Ohio).

> "I've dreamed about being at the line to win a game like this, since I was a little kid. I'm so happy that I was able to do what I did for the seniors, this team, this program and all of our fans."
> — Morris Peterson

MSU defied the oddsmakers, who made it a two-point underdog against Kentucky, and proved virtually every national analyst wrong by advancing from the toughest of the four regionals.

"When we talked about winning this game and getting to the Final Four, everybody laughed at us," Cleaves said. "But we're the ones hugging, dancing and crying right now because we've just done something that every kid who has ever dribbled a basketball dreams about."

Peterson sealed the team's trip to St. Petersburg by making six straight free throws in the final 28.9 seconds.

"I wasn't nervous," he said. "But a lot of stuff was running through my head. I've dreamed about being at the line to win a game like this, since I was a little kid. I'm so happy that I was able to do what I did for the seniors, this team, this program and all of our fans.

"I also didn't want to miss because I didn't want Antonio yelling at me again."

Antonio Smith and Andre Hutson celebrate the win over Kentucky.

Road to the Final Four
4th ROUND
NCAA

MSU 73, Kentucky 66

NCAA Midwest Regional Final
March 20, 1999 Trans World Dome, St. Louis

Kentucky	36	30	—	66
MSU	35	38	—	73

Kentucky (66)	min.	fg m-a	ft m-a	rb o-t	a	pf	tp
Evans	20	5-10	0-0	4-6	1	4	12
Padgett	30	3-8	3-5	1-3	2	4	11
Bradley	12	2-4	0-0	2-4	0	0	4
Turner	35	2-8	1-2	1-2	8	1	5
Allison	23	3-8	1-7	1-2	2	1	7
S. Smith	13	0-1	0-0	0-1	0	1	0
Prince	24	3-3	4-4	1-2	1	2	12
Hogan	6	1-2	0-0	1-3	1	0	2
Camara	11	2-4	0-0	0-0	0	0	4
Maglorie	26	3-5	3-4	0-1	0	3	9
Totals	200	24-53	12-16	11-24	15	16	66

Percentages: FG-.453, FT-.750. 3-Point Goals: 6-16, .375 (Evans 2-2, Prince 2-2, Padgett 2-6, S. Smith 0-1, Alison 0-2, Turner 0-3). Turnovers: 9. Steals: 5.

Michigan State (73)	min.	fg m-a	ft m-a	rb o-t	a	pf	tp
A Smith	33	1-2	2-2	1-7	0	2	4
Hutson	29	6-10	2-4	2-5	1	3	14
Klein	18	1-6	0-0	1-1	0	3	3
Cleaves	37	4-11	0-0	0-4	11	0	10
Bell	27	3-5	0-0	1-3	2	3	7
Kelley	2	1-1	0-2	0-0	0	0	2
Davis	3	0-0	0-0	0-0	2	0	0
Peterson	33	6-13	7-8	9-10	1	3	19
Granger	18	4-5	3-3	1-2	0	2	14
Totals	200	26-53	14-17	15-32	17	16	73

Percentages: FG-.491, FT-.824. 3-Point Goals: 7-17, .412 (Granger 3-3, Cleaves 2-5, Bell 1-2, Klein 1-5, Peterson 0-2). Turnovers: 11. Steals: 4.

Attendance: 42,519

DUKE 68, MSU 62

Road to the Final Four

Final Four

NCAA

AGONY OF ST. PETE

MARCH 28, 1999
TODD SCHULZ

Final Four

ST. PETERSBURG—The defense, suffocating all season, wasn't tight enough.

The rebounds, usually snatched with sure hands, fell to the enemy.

The second-half comeback, which had become tradition, never culminated.

The dream, which captivated a state, died at the hands of dominant Duke here Saturday night.

Michigan State's basketball team fell 68-62 to the Blue Devils in the Final Four of the NCAA Tournament at Tropicana Field.

The closest the Spartans got to Duke in the second half was three points.

"We were one or two plays from pulling it off," said Mateen Cleaves, MSU's All-American point guard. "You get so close. You can feel yourselves coming back. But we never got over the hump."

MSU finished the season 33-5, the most victories in school history. The Spartans reached the Final Four for the first time in 20 years and just the third time in 100 seasons.

"It's been a marvelous season," said Earvin "Magic" Johnson, the former NBA star and hero of MSU's 1979 NCAA title team. "For everybody who got here, this is the ultimate. We can't be sad."

The Spartans never led against the nation's No. 1-ranked Blue Devils (37-1), who play for the national title. The Huskies defeated Ohio State in Saturday's first semifinal, 64-58.

Duke is chasing its third national crown in the 1990s. Beating MSU was a major obstacle, coach Mike Krzyzewski said.

"We beat a great basketball team today in a great game," Krzyzewski said. "We are ultimately proud."

MSU boasted about 10,000 of the 41,340 fans who filled the palm-tree ringed arena Saturday. Most were packed into the northwest corner of the dome.

Before the tip-off, rowdy MSU students batted a beach ball and waved signs saying "I bleed green" and "We believe."

The sea of green was speckled with celebrities such as Johnson, former MSU coach Jud Heathcote, Gov. John Engler, San Francisco 49ers coach Steve Mariucci, U.S. Sen. Spencer Abraham and former MSU football and baseball star Kirk Gibson.

"Clearly, we are on center stage," MSU President Peter McPherson said.

Gibson, ever the ferocious competitor, looked ready to take the floor with the Spartans.

"This is what it's all about," said Gibson, sporting his trademark scruffy face. "This is the measuring stick."

MSU could have used Gibson early. Duke bolted to a 9-2 lead as Elton Brand—the national player of the year—scored six points and William Avery drained a 3-pointer. As they have all tournament, the Spartans rallied, cutting the lead to 9-8 on a 3-pointer from Cleaves.

But Duke continued to pound away inside, leading 20-10, 26-16 and 30-20 when Shane Battier muscled home a layup with less than five minutes left in the half. MSU, which made just nine of 31 shots in the first half and was outrebounded by a 2-to-1

MSU'S Mateen Cleaves drives the ball past Duke's William Avery.

margin, trailed 32-20 at the break.

"They just pounded us on the boards," MSU coach Tom Izzo said. "Every time we missed a shot, they got it. That's been our game all year."

Fans such as Johnson were frustrated.

"This is the game we wanted," Johnson said. "We played excellent defense. But we've blown it on the offensive glass and we've been tentative on offense." The Spartans stormed out in the second half with a 10-4 run, cutting Duke's lead to 36-30 on Antonio Smith's rebound and dunk with 16 minutes left.

MSU kept coming, trailing by seven when Cleaves hit a 3-pointer and just four—43-39—when Thomas Kelly scored on a putback with 13:24 left.

But Duke kept the Spartans at arm's length, mainly on Brand's baskets inside. The sophomore led all scorers with 18 points.

With Brand on the bench in foul trouble, MSU closed to 51-48 when Morris Peterson tipped home a hoop and Charlie Bell hit two free throws with eight minutes remaining.

Again, Duke answered. Trajan Langdon and Avery nailed 3-pointers and Avery scored again, pushing the lead back to 59-50.

"Their All-Americans stepped up," Izzo said. "That's why they're the No. 1 team in the nation. They made the big plays. We didn't."

The Spartans couldn't get closer than three points the rest of the way. They watched helplessly as the Blue Devils padded their lead with free throws in the final minutes.

"The guys fought valiantly," said Cleaves' mother, Fran. "We got here. We beat the odds. Maybe this will mean Mateen will definitely be back."

Cleaves, a junior, is considering leaving MSU early for the NBA. Should he return, MSU might be a favorite to reach the Final Four again.

"I'm about 80 percent sure he'll return," Fran Cleaves said. "But I'll leave that up to him."

MSU's Antonio Smith and Doug Davis surround Duke star Trajan Langdon.

As Spartan fans filed slowly out of the dome, they tried to focus on the positives of a record-setting season.

"We couldn't ask for anything more," said Chris Mundy, a 1996 MSU graduate. "Duke is a superior team. At every turning point, they hit the key baskets. What can you do?"· Michelle Wright, a 1995 MSU graduate, said Saturday's loss shouldn't tarnish a sparkling season.

"Duke earned it," she said. "We gave them a game. It's still satisfying to get this far."

Road to the Final Four

Final Four

NCAA

The Spartans gather in a huddle on the court at the start of the game against Duke.

Although MSU's season ended just short of its final goal, the 1998-99 Spartans still gave their fans ONE SHINING SEASON.

Road to the Final Four

Final Four

SPARTANS COMPLETE YEAR WITHOUT SHAME

MARCH 28, 1999
JACK EBLING

ST. PETERSBURG—Sometimes the other team is just better. Play golf against Tiger Woods and you'd better make a bunch of birdies.

Pitch to Mark McGwire and you'd better hope he swings at bad pitches.

And try to beat this year's Duke Blue Devils in the Final Four and you'd better be a few plays from perfect.

The Michigan State Spartans were a few plays from scoreless and perfectly awful on the boards in the first half Saturday.

So despite a terrific second-half effort, Tom Izzo's record-smashing team suffered its second six-point loss to one of the five best college teams I've seen.

To a 37-1 team that won't make as many mistakes Monday against Connecticut.

"If we played them 10 times, we might beat them a couple—at least once," Izzo said after a 68-62 setback. "They have so many weapons. And they went right at our strengths. . . . But they knew they were in a game."

> "They have a great team. And when you have a great team, someone will always step up. They proved why they're the No. 1 team in the country."

For the first 20 minutes, it was Player of the Year Elton Brand vs. Brand X.

But when a 12-point halftime lead was chopped to three, Duke did what champions do, answering that challenge with a 3-point shot from an All-American, Trajan Langdon.

It didn't matter that Langdon was 2-for-8 at that point and 0-for-3 from long range.

When his team had to plug a leak, he did the same thing MSU All-American Mateen Cleaves had done so often.

He plugged a shot and kept his team from feeling the way the damp-eyed Spartans did in a somber locker room.

They knew the Blue Devils were beatable with 14-for-27 work at the foul line, three more turnovers and five fewer assists.

Izzo's players also knew they'd blown a rare opportunity by being outrebounded 28-14 in the first half and hitting 4 of 18 shots from long range.

"They were killing us down low and with offensive rebounds," MSU shooting guard Charlie Bell said. "They have a great team. And when you have a great team, someone will always step up. They proved why they're the No. 1 team in the country."

The Spartans proved why they're No. 2 by giving Duke everything it wanted—including a shot at its third national title in nine years.

But there are no moral victories at this point for a program that has to beat the Blue Devils, as it did the Kentucky Wildcats, to reach the goals everyone shares.

"I think we really expected to win it all this year," MSU forward A.J. Granger said. "Last year was such a Cinderella season. We were just happy to be there. But that wasn't true this time."

No one was happy when the winningest season in Big Ten history ended at 33-5 and a school-record winning streak ended at 22 games.

A strong second half couldn't undo the damage that already had been done any more than it could make some idiots back home behave in a rational way.

The Spartans had more than their share of open shots, with Cleaves, Jason Klein, Thomas Kelley and Morris Peterson missing badly and often.

It isn't often a team can do as much as MSU did the past 12 weeks and leave feeling as empty as it did.

This, too, shall pass.

The team we'll remember was the one we saw in St. Louis last Sunday.

The memory Spartan players will have will be shaded by coming so close on a night they could have done what few thought possible.

"I really felt they were beatable," Peterson said. "But we got away from the things that got us here. They played harder than us in the first half. And that's the biggest disappointment. We came here to win."

Not to beat the point spread, to hear "Good try!" or to wonder how it might have been different.

Only two ways—by playing better or playing a different team.

Antonio Smith and Tom Izzo hug after Smith fouled at the end of the game against Duke.

Road to the Final Four

Final Four

NCAA

REVELERS OUT EARLY TO CHEER SPARTANS

MARCH 28, 1999

EAST LANSING—A combination of Spartan and spring fever gripped East Lansing all day Saturday.

Along Grand River Avenue, pregame partiers began to gather on restaurant patios and in bars as early as noon for the Final Four matchup between Michigan State and Duke eight hours later. A sea of smiles and MSU t-shirts greeted one of the area's first winter reprieves.

The smiles disappeared later as Duke ended the Spartans' dream season, 68-62.

But even before the game, loyal fans had just one thing to say: Thanks.

"It's an amazing team," said Lara Pevzner, an MSU senior, as she waited in line at Harper's in downtown East Lansing. "Thanks for this amazing basketball team."

At the Peanut Barrel, graduate students Hilary Moore and Bryan Vickstrom waited five hours for the game to start. "This game is going to justify my choice of graduate schools," said Vickstrom, who chose MSU over Duke.

About 3,000 filled Munn Arena to watch the game on a large-screen TV.

They erupted in cheers of "Go Green, Go White." MSU officials tossed out at least 600 t-shirts that read, "A season to remember: '99."

Megan Hinterman, an MSU sophomore, went to the arena with five friends. "The crowd is so amazing when they're all together like this," she said.

Morris Peterson's sister, Tonda, cheers for her brother and his Spartan teammates at the Final Four.

MSU Overall Statistics—1998-99

OVERALL RECORD: 33-5
BIG TEN RECORD: 15-1 (1ST PLACE)

	GP-GS	MIN. AVG.	FG PCT.	3-PT. PCT.	FT PCT.	REBOUNDS OFF	TOT	AVG.	PF	A	TO	BLK	ST	PTS. AVG.
42 Peterson, Morris	38-4	23.9	.554	.373	.814	92	216	5.7	97	36	62	22	33	13.6
12 Cleaves, Mateen	38-38	31.2	.406	.292	.787	12	62	1.6	78	274	141	2	69	11.7
44 Klein, Jason	37-37	23.1	.413	.338	.786	50	99	3.7	38	36	30	3	34	9.4
34 Hutson, Andre	37-34	25.0	.617	.000	.761	89	198	5.2	100	33	53	32	36	8.9
14 Bell, Charlie	38-34	22.7	.477	.366	.754	78	146	3.8	85	39	43	3	27	7.8
43 Granger, A.J.	38-5	20.7	.532	.500	.714	64	147	3.9	64	22	44	17	21	6.6
13 Smith, Antonio	38-37	29.1	.535	.000	.462	105	319	8.4	104	41	71	12	56	6.5
3 Kelley, Thomas	36-1	15.0	.360	.286	.833	15	46	1.7	45	51	45	5	34	5.1
30 Davis, Doug	38-0	7.4	.391	.371	.476	3	19	0.5	32	42	22	6	8	1.9
55 Ballinger, Adam	4-0	5.5	1.000	.000	.000	0	5	1.3	2	1	2	3	1	1.5
5 Guess, Lorenzo	13-0	2.5	.500	.500	.000	5	8	0.6	0	0	4	0	0	0.8
25 Cherry, Steve	17-0	1.6	.400	.000	.500	2	7	0.4	3	2	3	0	1	0.5
23 Smith, Brandon	12-0	1.8	.250	.000	.500	0	1	0.1	1	2	5	0	2	0.3
15 Ishbia, Matt	0-0	0.0	.000	.000	.000	0	0	0.0	0	0	0	0	0	0.0
11 Thomas, David	0-0	0.0	.000	.000	.000	0	0	0.0	0	0	0	0	0	0.0
10 Schembrl, Tony	0-0	0.0	.000	.000	.000	.000	0	0.0	0	0	0	0	0	0.0
Team Rebounds						56	112							
MICHIGAN STATE	38		.474	.340	.733	563	1379	36.3	689	569	533	100	298	71.7
OPPONENTS	38		.426	.319	.693	366	1031	27.1	682	412	587	107	240	59.5